To

....

From

....

Date

....

Published by Barbour Publishing, Inc., 1810 Barbour Drive, Uhrichsville, Ohio 44683, www.barbourbooks.com

Our mission is to inspire the world with the life-changing message of the Bible.

 Member of the
Evangelical Christian
Publishers Association

Printed in the United States of America.

Sandra Harner

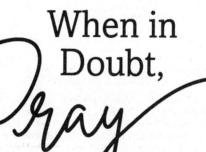

When in Doubt,

Pray

Devotional Prayers

for Women

BARBOUR
PUBLISHING

Introduction

When we are experiencing trials and difficulties, doubts can begin assailing us, picking away at our peace, pulling us away from God, waiting to trip us up and out of His will for our lives. That's when we need to pick up our Bible and read the truth found in God's Word. Then we will be filled with the certainty that He does indeed see what we're going through. That He is ready to come alongside and help us through our challenges. That He is eager to have us come to Him in prayer, seeking His presence, comfort, love, and calm, and receiving all He has to give us.

This devotional has been written for you—to help you erase any doubts you may be entertaining about your worth, God's love for you, your gifts and abilities, your faith, His promises, your influence in this world, your future, and the fact that He does indeed hear your prayers. In each reading, you will find scripture verses relating to each topic, as well as a prayer for you to present to God.

May you find encouragement as you read each page, meditate upon each syllable of God's Word, then present your petition to Him, allowing Him speak to your heart and soul as you offer up each prayer to His listening ear.

When You Doubt

Your Worth

· ·

*You, beloved, are worth so much more
than a whole flock of sparrows.*
Matthew 10:31 voice

In the Very Image of God

So God created man in his own image, in the
image of God he created him; male and female
he created them. And God blessed them.
GENESIS 1:27–28 ESV

. . . .

Dear Lord, some days I wonder about my worthiness. When I look at myself through my own eyes, I see how much I must fall short in Yours. Too often, it seems, I find myself faltering, doubting, and making a misstep.

Yet then Your Holy Spirit draws me to Your Word. Within its pages, I am reminded that I'm made in Your very image. That I am more valuable than I could ever hope or imagine. That because You treasure me, You sacrificed Your Son so that I could draw ever closer to You.

You knew me, a child of Eve, while I was still in my mother's womb. Then, when I entered this world, You breathed Your breath of life into me. You have promised to take care of me. To be my "God forever," my "guide till the end of time" (Psalm 48:14 MSG).

Lord, help me to rest in that knowledge. To understand that, because I am Your child, I am worthy of Your help, provision, and love! Help me to see my value through Your eyes, not mine or the world's. In Jesus' name, I live and pray, amen.

More Than Sparrows

Your Father in heaven knows when those small sparrows fall to the ground. You, beloved, are worth so much more than a whole flock of sparrows. God knows everything about you, even the number of hairs on your head. So do not fear.

MATTHEW 10:29–31 VOICE

Dear Lord, how can I be worthy of Your salvation, Your love, Your grace? Every day I fall short of Your glory. I say words I later regret. I leap before I think. My thoughts at times turn dark. I envy those whose lives seem better or happier than mine. I turn in fear instead of turning to You. Those are the times when I begin to wonder how I can even begin to be worth all that You have done for me.

Yet, Lord, Your Word tells me two sparrows are only worth a penny, and You care for them. Not one falls to the ground without Your notice. Not one feather gets caught up by the wind without Your seeing it. Then You tell me that I am worth so much more than an entire flock of sparrows. You say You know how many hairs are on my head. I am humbled and achingly grateful that You treasure me. Thank You, Lord. In Jesus' name I pray, amen.

Everlasting Life

"God so [greatly] loved and dearly prized the world,
that He [even] gave His [One and] only begotten Son,
so that whoever believes and trusts in Him [as Savior]
shall not perish, but have eternal life. For God did not
send the Son into the world to judge and condemn the
world [that is, to initiate the final judgment of the world],
but that the world might be saved through Him."

JOHN 3:16–17 AMP

. . . .

Dear Lord, Your love for Your children, for *me*, is amazing. For each and every one of us, You sacrificed Your one and only Son so that we might have life, a life that lasts forever.

You paid such an incredible price to ensure that I could come to You, run to You. Because I am that important to You, I long to show myself worthy of Your great gift. Help me do that by becoming an obedient child, one who loves as Your Son loves. Help me to remove myself from my throne and permit You to become the Lord of my life and my love. To honor You each and every day in all I say and do. In the sweet and precious name of Jesus I pray, amen.

The Gift of God

It's by God's grace that you have been saved.
You receive it through faith. It was not our plan or
our effort. It is God's gift, pure and simple. You
didn't earn it, not one of us did, so don't go around
bragging that you must have done something amazing.
EPHESIANS 2:8–9 VOICE

Lord, there are times when I think I'm not good enough to receive Your grace, that I must do something, work to earn it. Yet then Your Word opens up my heart to the fact that there is nothing I need to do to receive Your grace—except to believe, to have faith that You have actually gifted to me this grace. That there's nothing I can do to earn what You have already done. That I cannot even claim that my faith comes from my own efforts but comes from You alone.

May I return Your love and mercy by standing in the fore "as a living testimony to the incredible riches of [Your] grace and kindness" (Ephesians 2:7 VOICE) on this side of heaven. May I return Your gift of faith by becoming a light that shines in the darkness, one that draws others to You. May I praise You for giving me beyond what I could ever hope for or imagine. Amen.

A Centurion's Faith

*Jesus went with them. But just before they arrived
at the house, the officer sent some friends to say,
"Lord, don't trouble yourself by coming to my home,
for I am not worthy of such an honor. I am not even
worthy to come and meet you. Just say the word from
where you are, and my servant will be healed."*
Luke 7:6–7 NLT

. . . .

Lord, my prayer life lacks luster. Part of that comes from an error in thinking that I am not worthy enough to enter Your presence. So I try to fix things in my own way, under my own power. Then, when I come to the end of myself and my efforts, I look to You, more in desperation than hope.

Help me change my mindset, Lord. Help me to understand that You care about every little thing that is going on in my life. That You would like nothing more than for me to come to You, to talk to You, to ask You to heal those I treasure in their earthly existence. Remind me that all You need to do is hear my prayer, say perhaps one word from wherever You are, and my answer will be winging its way into my life.

Help me to come to You, knowing that You deem me worthy enough to enter Your presence, no matter the time or the problem. There is no distance You cannot breach. Amen.

Special to God

*I, the Eternal One, am your God. I am the Holy One
of Israel, and I will save you. I have traded in nations
to win you back, Egypt, Cush, and Seba, in exchange
for your freedom. Because you are special to Me and
I love you, I gladly give up other peoples in exchange
for you; they are trivial by comparison to your
weighty significance. So don't be afraid. I am here.*
ISAIAH 43:3–5 VOICE

Often, Lord, I feel anything but special. Most times, I feel like it's me against this world. But then You urge me into Your Word, and I read passages about how special I am to You. How much You love me and would give up others so that You could have me alone.

Remembering that I am precious in Your sight lifts me up from my doldrums and into Your amazing and awesome presence. Your love and care for me boosts my courage. Knowing You are not just standing beside me on the good days but walking with me through raging floodwaters, ensuring I will not lose my footing and be taken by the current; knowing that You are with me amid the fire, ensuring I will not get burned, lifts me higher than I ever dreamed imaginable.

Knowing You have named me as Your very own, that You have chosen me, warms my heart and banishes all chaos. In You, I find my love, my life, my calm. Amen.

Heart Smart

*Samuel took one look at Eliab and thought, "Surely
this is the LORD's anointed!" But the LORD said to
Samuel, "Don't judge by his appearance or height,
for I have rejected him. The LORD doesn't see things
the way you see them. People judge by outward
appearance, but the LORD looks at the heart."*
1 SAMUEL 16:6–7 NLT

At times, Lord, I look in the mirror and see a woman of little value.
My features are so much less than perfect. My weight is not where
I'd like it to be. My hair is dull, my teeth misaligned. Need I go on?
The point is, sometimes I look in the mirror and wonder why You
would choose me to be a part of Your eternal kingdom.

And then I turn to Your Word and read what You told Samuel
when he was looking at Jesse's sons and trying to find which one
You wanted to be anointed as the next king. It was then You made
the point that You don't look at Your children like other people do.
You don't judge by outward appearance but by one's heart.

Help me to remember that, Lord, when I consider my value to
You. It is You alone I want to please. It is to You alone that I offer my
heart, spirit, and soul. In Jesus' name, amen.

Working for God's Glory

Each one's work will be clearly shown [for what it is];
for the day [of judgment] will disclose it, because it is
to be revealed with fire, and the fire will test the quality
and character and worth of each person's work.
1 CORINTHIANS 3:13 AMP

In the end, Father, You will be the judge of my lifetime of work; and I know You don't care if I work behind a cash register or an oak desk with a five-line telephone. It's not what I do that matters, but how I do it. Am I a cheerful worker? Am I an honest worker? Am I a worker whose love for You is evident in what I say and how I treat my fellow workers? Do I care more for my brothers and sisters than for my next paycheck? I am Your ambassador, Lord; and every day I try to show Your love to those who do not know You. I pray that when the time comes, You will find me worthy. In Jesus' name, amen.

Restorative Justice

All have turned away; together they've become worthless.
No one does good, not even one. . . . But now for the
good news: God's restorative justice has entered the
world, independent of the law. . . . This expression of
God's restorative justice displays in the present that
He is just and righteous and that He makes right
those who trust and commit themselves to Jesus.
ROMANS 3:12, 21, 26 VOICE

We humans failed, Lord, when we tried to follow Your laws. Even though You gave us those parameters, guidelines You set up so that we would know how to live—even then, we fell so short of who and what You wanted us to be and do. But then You presented us with the good news of Jesus Christ, the being, the Son whose death restored justice and made us—those who trust in and commit themselves to Him—right in Your eyes.

For putting up with us, I thank You, Lord. For sending Your loyal Son to earth to die on our behalf so that we could live, I will be forever grateful. Thank You for making us right in Your eyes. Amen.

Unforgotten

Zion (Jerusalem in captivity) said, "The Lord has
abandoned me, and my Lord has forgotten me." [The
Lord answered] "Can a woman forget her nursing child
and have no compassion on the son of her womb? Even
these may forget, but I will not forget you. Indeed, I have
inscribed [a picture of] you on the palms of My hands."
Isaiah 49:14–16 amp

There are times, Lord, when I feel not just unworthy but hopeless. Forgotten. Just one more speck of flotsam adrift in the sea. But then I read passages like this one. And I remember.

I remember that I might have bad days. But I can brighten them by keeping Your truth in my mind and heart. The truth that You will never abandon me. That You will never forget me. That I am always on Your mind and in Your heart.

For You make me realize, put it in the forefront of my mind, that just as a good mother can never forget or stop loving a child of her womb, You, a good Father, will never forget or stop loving me. You will always look upon me with compassion, wanting to help me, heal me, hold me. And the fact that You even have a picture of me etched upon the palms of Your hands makes my heart soar.

In You I find my life. In You I find my purpose. In You I find my hope. Amen.

Known and Loved

O LORD, you have searched me [thoroughly] and have known me. You know when I sit down and when I rise up [my entire life, everything I do]; You understand my thought from afar. You scrutinize my path and my lying down, and You are intimately acquainted with all my ways. Even before there is a word on my tongue [still unspoken], behold, O LORD, You know it all.
PSALM 139:1–4 AMP

Lord, You know everything about me. Even my most secret thoughts and longings. You know what I do when and where and why. You see me when I stand, sit, or lie down. Nothing about me is hidden from Your eyes or heart. And still You love me.

You, Lord, love me even when I'm having trouble loving myself. Help me to remember that when I get down on myself, when I think nothing I do matters, when I consider myself an unimportant cog in this wheel called life.

Master Creator, You designed me. You put me here for a purpose. Help me to always remember that because You deem me worthy, I am to consider myself of value to You. Today and every day, from here to eternity. Amen.

The Temple

Don't you realize that your body is the temple of the Holy
Spirit, who lives in you and was given to you by God?
You do not belong to yourself, for God bought you with
a high price. So you must honor God with your body.

1 CORINTHIANS 6:19–20 NLT

In the days of yore, women were often bought and sold, treated more like chattel than a living, breathing human being of value. That was once, and in some places still is, the earthly perception of women. But You, Lord, have another point of view.

You have used Your daughters as Your first evangelists, to spread the joy and wonder of Your Word becoming our reality. You also honored us by paying for our souls and spirits at an unbelievable cost to You—the life of Your one and only Son.

In return, Father, help me to remember that both You *and* Jesus paid a tremendous price for me. That You have blessed me by allowing me to be a vessel housing Your gift of the Holy Spirit. That I am to honor You with my body by using it for Your glory, not my shame.

May I thank You every day for allowing me and my sisters to be a part of Your plan and promises. In Jesus' love and name I pray, amen.

In This Place

*Then Jacob awoke from his sleep and said, "Surely
the LORD is in this place, and I wasn't even aware
of it!" But he was also afraid and said, "What an
awesome place this is! It is none other than the
house of God, the very gateway to heaven."*
GENESIS 28:16–17 NLT

There are times, Lord, when I'm not proud of what I've done. That's when I go on the run. But the good news is that no matter what I've done, no matter where I go, You still love and value me. You still want me to be a part of Your divine plan.

Just like You met Jacob on the run from his brother, Esau, in the wilderness, Lord, I ask You to meet me in mine. Speak to me through Your Word, Your visions of the night. Remind me that You are wherever I go, watching over me, keeping me safe, and that You will bring me back to where You would have me be.

Help me remember that I need never be alone when I trust in, hope for, and look to You for peace and provision. For Your angels will surround me, and You will guard me in the darkness and light. In Jesus' name, amen.

Already Blessed

I know I am not worthy of even a little of all of the loyal
love and faithfulness You have shown to me, Your servant.
You have already blessed me because I left home and
crossed the Jordan with nothing except my staff. Now
I have grown into two large camps. Rescue me now.
GENESIS 32:10–11 VOICE

Lord, You have promised me good in my life. Yet I feel I am unworthy of Your love for and commitment to me. You know how many mistakes I have made, how often I have spoken and wounded my listener, how many times I have fallen prey to temptation.

Yet no matter how imperfect I am and may become, You still bless my life. You still answer my prayers. You still rescue me from the circumstances in which I become entangled.

And here I am again, Lord, coming to You, reminding You of how unworthy I must appear in Your eyes. Yet You look at me as Your servant, a woman of value, a woman You seek and continue to bless, whenever and wherever You find me.

When I come to You, looking for Your help in overcoming a challenge, help me not to bend to evil in fear but to rise up in confidence, knowing that You are with me and will bring only good into my life wherever I roam. Amen.

Homecoming

"When he came to himself, he said, 'How many of my
father's hired servants have more than enough bread,
but I perish here with hunger! I will arise and go to my
father, and I will say to him, "Father, I have sinned against
heaven and before you. I am no longer worthy to be called
your son. Treat me as one of your hired servants."'"

LUKE 15:17–19 ESV

• •

Lord, when I take what You have graciously blessed me with and go off on my own, attaching myself to the world, trouble inevitably follows. Yet, for some reason, You help me to come to myself. To realize in the midst of my misery that I have walked away from You.

It is then that I come running back, telling You I am not worthy to be Your daughter. But You pay my words no heed. Instead, You, whose eyes are always looking for me, run to me. In Your compassion and grace, Your love and affection, You enfold me in Your arms. You turn from my confession and begin shouting orders in preparation for my homecoming party.

For Your watchful eye, gracious gifts, unending and unconditional love and compassion, for Your eternal kiss, I thank You. In Jesus' name, amen.

Rightly Handling the Word

Do your best to present yourself to God as one
approved, a worker who has no need to be
ashamed, rightly handling the word of truth.

2 TIMOTHY 2:15 ESV

Lord, when I pick up Your Holy Book, I'm awed that in my hands I hold the very God-breathed words with which You inspired the pens of others. I am delighted to know Your Word continues to uplift, guide, and direct Your children. To this day, readers may find Your Word dripping with love and compassion, and painstakingly revealing the plan You have given each soul and spirit.

Lord, Your Word is the truth, the light, and the way forward for me and countless others. As I read the passages, give me the wisdom I need so that I can discover Your path and handle Your Word in a way that would please You. Allow Your Holy Spirit to guide me through each scene and verse so I may share Your Word with others. Open my mind to Your understanding and my heart to Your voice.

Guide me where You would have me go. Show me what You would have me see. Tell me what You would have me share. Speak, Lord. I'm listening. In Jesus' name, amen.

Walk Worthy

*With each of you we were like a father with his child,
holding your hand, whispering encouragement, showing
you step-by-step how to live well before God, who called
us into his own kingdom, into this delightful life.*

1 THESSALONIANS 2:12 MSG

Lord, I want to live a life worthy of the one to which You have called me. To do that I need guidance as well as a thirst for the Word itself. So, Lord, I pray that I would be encouraged by Your Word. That it would be like my teacher, cheering me on, supporting me, cautioning me of the difficulties and stressors I might encounter.

I thank You for deeming me a woman worthy of this calling You have put upon my heart, spirit, soul, and mind. I thank You for this great privilege.

Now I would pray that Your Helper would play an even bigger role in my life so that I may navigate the course You have set before me, find the path You would have me follow, say the words You would have me speak and the song You would have me sing, be the woman You created me to be. Amen.

Emerging Victorious

Since we have a great High Priest, Jesus, the Son of God who has passed through the heavens from death into new life with God, let us hold tightly to our faith. For Jesus is not some high priest who has no sympathy for our weaknesses and flaws. He has already been tested in every way that we are tested; but He emerged victorious, without failing God.
HEBREWS 4:14–15 VOICE

Help me, Lord, to hold fast to my faith, to never waver in my trust in You. When times are difficult and the way seems dark, remind me that You were tested in every way that I myself am. And You didn't make a misstep.

Even though You walked the earth thousands of years before I did, You are familiar with all my pain, emotions, stressors, and frustrations. I pray that with Your help, I will be able to resist Satan's teasers. I pray that You will cover me with Your presence and remind me that You found me worthy of Your sacrifice on the cross.

Continue to reach down and touch my life. Help me to hold fast to that truth that because You were victorious, I can be victorious. That You believe in my worth, even when I have my own doubts. That You love me even when I feel unlovable. That when I'm ready to give up, You will give me the hope and strength to carry on. Amen.

Finding Those Worthy

"Whatever city or village you enter, ask who in it is worthy
[who welcomes you and your message], and stay at his
house until you leave [that city]. As you go into the house,
give it your greeting [that is, 'Peace be to this house']. If
[the family living in] the house is worthy [welcoming you
and your message], give it your [blessing of] peace [that is,
a blessing of well-being and prosperity, the favor of God].
But if it is not worthy, take back your blessing of peace."
MATTHEW 10:11–13 AMP

Dear Lord, You encouraged Your disciples to let their peace fall upon a house where people are worthy—eager to grow in Your grace. But to seek out such people, to even begin such a journey, I must be ready and willing to share my message. Yet so many ideas about my own unworthiness keep me cowering in the corner.

Help me to remember, to get it through my head, that in Your eyes, I am worthy to follow, to love, to lead, to teach, to spread Your message. For the more worthy I believe I am to You, the more worthy I will appear in my own eyes and mind, increasing my confidence and courage.

So use me, Lord, to bless and be blessed by deeming myself worthy and carrying Your message of peace to others. Amen.

Worthy of a Living Hope

*Blessed [gratefully praised and adored] be the God
and Father of our Lord Jesus Christ, who according
to His abundant and boundless mercy has caused us
to be born again [that is, to be reborn from above—
spiritually transformed, renewed, and set apart for
His purpose] to an ever-living hope and confident
assurance through the resurrection of Jesus Christ
from the dead, [born anew] into an inheritance which
is imperishable [beyond the reach of change] and
undefiled and unfading, reserved in heaven for you.*

1 PETER 1:3–4 AMP

Lord, You reached out to me with Your saving grace and made me Your child—one who has been spiritually reborn in You. And all because Your Son died on the cross and rose again, defeating death and giving me a living hope.

It is You, Lord, who has declared me worthy of an inheritance that will never perish, that will never be defiled, that will never fade. This inheritance is kept in heaven for me. I thank You, Lord, for this living hope that You have given me. I thank You that in Your grace and mercy, You declared me worthy of this wondrous gift. Help me, Lord, to obey Your Word and to follow You on earth and into heaven. In Jesus' name I pray, amen.

So Beautiful

*You are so beautiful, my love, without blemish. Come
with me from Lebanon, my bride; come with me from
Lebanon. Journey with me from the crest of Amana,
from the top of Senir even the summit of Hermon,
from the lions' dangerous den, from the mountain
hideouts of leopards. My heart is your captive, my
sister, my bride; you have stolen it with one glance.*
SONG OF SOLOMON 4:7–9 VOICE

Dear Lord, it is hard to fathom the love You hold for me. In Your eyes, I am beautiful and perfect. But the world gives me a different story. To be worthy, I need to look like a supermodel. To only weigh so many pounds. To be well-educated, happily married, on an amazing career path. It seems that in the world's eyes, I will never be good enough.

Yet You love me in a way no other does. You call me *beautiful, Your love, without blemish.* You want to spend time with me, to take me places where I will be safe, loved, calmed, and delighted.

Help me to see myself and other believers the way You see me. Help me to remember that with You, in Your company, on Your path, I will be safe, sheltered, protected, loved beyond compare. In Jesus' name, amen.

Be Holy

*[Live] as obedient children [of God]; do not be conformed
to the evil desires which governed you in your ignorance
[before you knew the requirements and transforming
power of the good news regarding salvation]. But like
the Holy One who called you, be holy yourselves in
all your conduct [be set apart from the world by your
godly character and moral courage]; because it is
written, "YOU SHALL BE HOLY (set apart), FOR I AM HOLY."*
1 PETER 1:14–16 AMP

. . . .

Dear Lord, in the past, I was disobedient and ignorant of Your love because I knew nothing of Your grace and mercy, nothing about a Holy God. But then You called me, considered me worthy to be called to become like You, to walk in Your will and way.

Lord, it is only through Your grace and mercy that I can be holy, just as You are. So I ask You, Lord, to help me follow Your example. To not slip up and fall back into my old ways.

Use Your Word, Lord, to transform me into the woman You created me to be. Help me to have the courage to walk away from what no longer serves me and to walk into the path You set before me. For I long to be holy as You are holy. Amen.

A Credit to God

May their lives be a credit to You, Lord; and what's
more, may they continue to delight You by doing
every good work and growing in the true knowledge
that comes from being close to You. Strengthen them
with Your infinite power, according to Your glorious
might, so that they will have everything they need to
hold on and endure hardship patiently and joyfully.

COLOSSIANS 1:10–11 VOICE

Dear Lord, I want to be a credit to You. To aid me in my efforts, I ask You to show me what pleases You, to make clear how I am to love You with all my heart, mind, and soul, and in what manner I am to love my neighbor as myself.

As I learn how to please You, to love others as I do You, I feel certain I will be bearing precious fruit for You. With You at the center of all I am and do, I know You will supply me with the power and strength to do what You would have me do. Through Your Word, You will give me what I need to grow, become patient, and find joy.

Direct me and use me, Lord. May I bathe everything I do in Your holy name. And may my knowledge and love of You increase as I follow You. Amen.

Renewed and Worthy

*You know to take off your former way of life, your
crumpled old self—that dark blot of a soul corrupted
by deceitful desire and lust—to take a fresh breath and
to let God renew your attitude and spirit. Then you
are ready to put on your new self, modeled after the
very likeness of God: truthful, righteous, and holy.*
EPHESIANS 4:22–24 VOICE

Lord, when You saved me from sin and put a new heart within me, I began to see things in a new light—*Your* light. Having met You and confessed my faith in You, I took off my old self and became a new creature. You have made me anew.

Help me, Father God, to become more like Your Son, Jesus, each and every day. To speak the truth. To be a woman of kindness and love, always keeping in mind that "we are all part of one another" (Ephesians 4:25 VOICE). To see that everyone around me is just as worthy as I to be or become Your child. To not allow my anger to rule me, nor to give the devil a foothold in my life.

I thank You, Lord, for giving me the time and room to become who You originally created me to be—a daughter of God. Continue to renew my spirit and mind. In Jesus' name I pray, amen.

Worthy of Your Calling

*I want you to get out there and walk—better yet,
run!—on the road God called you to travel. I don't
want any of you sitting around on your hands. I don't
want anyone strolling off, down some path that goes
nowhere. And mark that you do this with humility and
discipline—not in fits and starts, but steadily, pouring
yourselves out for each other in acts of love, alert at
noticing differences and quick at mending fences.*
Ephesians 4:1–3 MSG

Dear Lord, I want to live a life worthy of the calling You have extended to me. This will take some eagerness on my part.

This road You have given me to travel may have some false starts, some bumps, perhaps even last-minute lurching. But no matter what comes my way, keep me on Your path—the one that leads to You.

Make me a humble traveler, not one that sits on the roadside and brags and boasts about how far I have come or how much I accomplished in my own strength. Make me one who acknowledges that it is only by Your grace, strength, and power that I am the woman I am today.

Give me a heart filled with love that spills over into my actions. Make me a woman of peace. A woman living a life worthy of her calling. Amen.

From Beginning to End

And I am sure of this, that he who began a good work in
you will bring it to completion at the day of Jesus Christ.
PHILIPPIANS 1:6 ESV

Dear God, from the day that I asked You to be my Savior and Lord, I have wondered if I was worthy to claim You as my own. I wondered if I was worthy to receive all Your blessings and promises. And then I discover Your Word telling me that You, who began this good work in me, will continue to grow me. You will continue to guide me so that when You are ready to return, I will be found complete.

Lord, I thank You that You work daily in my life. For Your Spirit that speaks to my spirit and teaches me Your Word. This same Spirit brings me comfort and peace when I am going through difficult times. You have promised that He will guard me and keep me until the day You return.

So, Lord, while I know I am imperfect and have lots to learn, I also know that You will not stop working on me but keep perfecting my design. This knowledge gives me the strength, hope, and confidence to keep going. In Jesus' name, amen.

When You Doubt

God's Love for You

. . . .

*May you have the power to understand, as
all God's people should, how wide, how
long, how high, and how deep his love is.
May you experience the love of Christ.*
EPHESIANS 3:18–19 NLT

Love like Christ

*"A new commandment I give to you, that you love
one another: just as I have loved you, you also are to
love one another. By this all people will know that you
are my disciples, if you have love for one another."*
JOHN 13:34—35 ESV

Dear Lord, I often wonder how You could love me, for in my own eyes, I so often fall short of all that You would have me be and do. Too much of the time I find myself wrapped up in the things of this world. So I kneel before You in prayer and ask You to help me turn from worldly idols and embrace You alone as my God and King.

Help me to love my fellow humans just as You love me. Remind me not to judge or criticize others, to not tear them down but build them up with words of encouragement, doing for them what You and Your Word do for me. Teach me how to forgive the wrongs done to me, to forgive as You have forgiven me.

May I, in my love, reflect Your love to this world so that others will be attracted to the love and light You so willingly shine upon me. Amen.

My Rescuing Knight

I love you, GOD—you make me strong. GOD is bedrock
under my feet, the castle in which I live, my rescuing
knight. My God—the high crag where I run for dear life,
hiding behind the boulders, safe in the granite hideout.

PSALM 18:1–2 MSG

Lord of love, You are my knight in shining armor, my rock, my fortress, and my deliverer. You are the strength I need to begin the day and the calm I need at night. Help me to trust You always—to rest in Your protection and the peace Your hideout affords.

You are the bedrock upon which I stand, upon which I build my life. You are the impenetrable castle that shields me from the stinging arrows of misfortune.

You, Lord, are the high place to which I can run when I am afraid, worried, confused, desperate, and unsure. Keep me safe in Your arms, under Your protection, until I am able to rise up once more, with You right beside me, whispering words of encouragement and confidence.

Grace me with the fortitude to live Your Word, walk Your way, and speak Your truth. Today and every day I pray in the name and strength of Jesus, my rescuer, my eternal strength, my knight with whom I plan to live happily ever after. Amen.

The Personification of Love

Love is from God; and everyone who loves [others]
is born of God and knows God [through personal
experience]. The one who does not love has not
become acquainted with God [does not and never did
know Him], for God is love. [He is the originator of
love, and it is an enduring attribute of His nature.]
1 JOHN 4:7–8 AMP

. . . .

Dear God, You are the personification of the fountain, the source of all love. And because You love me, I am able to love all whom You put on my path.

When I dwell on these truths, I am overwhelmed by what You have done for me, dying on the cross for me, rescuing me from the darkness before I even knew You. You take my breath away.

Filled with the height and breadth of Your love, I pray You would help me love others, especially those who seem unlovely and unlovable. Make me a caring person, a good listener, one sensitive to the needs of others. Help me to help them and, in so doing, demonstrate the love You gave me before I really knew You.

Open my eyes so that I may see Your love every day. And when evening comes, I pray that I will rest, covered by and cocooned in Your overwhelming, everlasting, ever-giving love. Amen.

An Expression of Love

For God expressed His love for the world in this way: He
gave His only Son so that whoever believes in Him will not
face everlasting destruction, but will have everlasting life.
JOHN 3:16 VOICE

. . . .

Dear Lord, it's difficult to fathom how You could love a world that has rejected You time and time again. How could You love a people that grumbled, disobeyed, rebelled, and complained for forty years in the wilderness? What kept You coming back to dig Your people out of the trouble they'd gotten themselves into? Why did You put up with them, all their imperfections and shenanigans?

Although I may never understand the extent of Your love, I have read about how, no matter their being for or against You, You loved Your chosen people enough to leave a remnant to enter into the land of Your promises. Then thousands of years later, You loved humankind so much that You gave up Your only Son to save those who seemed so unworthy of Your love and His sacrifice!

Lord, in those times when I begin to doubt Your love, remind me what You have done for me and countless others. Lead me to accept the unfathomable depth of Your love and revel in it. Amen.

God's Love Manifest

In this the love of God was made manifest
among us, that God sent his only Son into the
world, so that we might live through him.
1 JOHN 4:9 ESV

. . . .

Lord, You sent Your only Son into the world, knowing full well that He would die a horrible death, and all so that I might live through Him. That grand and awesome truth is astonishing. And although You have shown Your love for me, for all Your people, in so many other and different ways, it is this supreme sacrifice that made Your love so evident.

May I, Lord, never doubt Your great love for me and mine. And although I can never make up for what happened to Your Son, I can make an effort to take one step closer to living through Him each and every day, to be accepting of Your great love, and to spread it where You would have it grow and flourish.

With Your help and love, Lord, I desire to live a godly life—one that reflects Your compassionate character. Show me how to do that every day by bringing to my mind, heart, spirit, and eyes the passages in Your Word that would help me walk Your way. Amen.

Everlasting Love

This is the way God put it: "They found grace out in the desert, these people who survived the killing. Israel, out looking for a place to rest, met God out looking for them!" God told them, "I've never quit loving you and never will. Expect love, love, and more love!"

JEREMIAH 31:2—3 MSG

Lord, when I begin to doubt Your love, take me back in my mind to the days when Your people were wandering in the desert, looking for a place to rest. And while they were looking, they found You looking for them!

When I feel lost, when I begin to doubt Your love, You remind me in Your Word that no matter what is happening in my life, You never quit loving me. And You never will. You make it clear that when I am lost, it's not *You* who has moved—it's *me*! When I am in despair or doubt, You remind me that not only are You always with me, but You're always loving me. And I can continually expect more and more of Your love!

You, Your Word, and Your love, Lord, are beyond what I can fathom. Lead me to rest in Your unending, ageless, constant love, the kind that brings light and chases away the darkness inside my heart. In that same everlasting love, I rejoice in the name of Jesus. Amen.

Love Dwelling Within

Jesus answered, "If anyone [really] loves Me, he will keep
My word (teaching); and My Father will love him, and We
will come to him and make Our dwelling place with him."

JOHN 14:23 AMP

Lord, these words scare me sometimes. The idea that only those who truly love You follow the course You have set out for them. There are so many times I feel I have fallen short, that I have deviated from Your way, that I have perhaps misunderstood Your Word. And then I wonder, *Have I lost God's love because I've made a misstep?*

Then I remember that Your Son has cleared the roadway for me. That because of His sacrifice, the eternal way will remain open to me, and no one can snatch me out of His hands.

Thus, I am assured that You and Your Son love me. You both, along with the Spirit, will make Your home in the deepest part of me.

Give me the strength, energy, and wisdom to be Your worthy abode, Lord. Each morning may I prepare to receive You, my divine guests, to walk Your way, live Your Truth, seek Your face, and receive Your everlasting and unsurpassing love. In Jesus' name I pray, amen.

Completely Filled

May you experience the love of Christ, though it is too
great to understand fully. Then you will be made complete
with all the fullness of life and power that comes from God.
EPHESIANS 3:19 NLT

Lord, although I may not understand everything about Your amazing love for me and all those for whom You sacrificed everything, I can open my heart more fully so that I may experience Your love more and more with each passing moment, hour, day. It is Your love I strive to receive, to allow in, to fill me unencumbered. So help me, Lord, to allow Your presence in my life to erode away any obstacles that may present a barrier, stopping Your love from streaming in, from filling me up heart, mind, soul, spirit. Help me to turn away from any doubts I may have, to acknowledge the power and enormity of Your love, to understand and believe that Your love can burn away any misgivings, misunderstandings, missteps of which I am ashamed.

Lord, God of my heart, fill me up throughout my being so that I may be "completely filled and flooded with God Himself" (Ephesians 3:19 AMP). In Jesus' name and love I pray, amen.

God Is Love

*Beloved, let us love one another, for love is from
God, and whoever loves has been born of God
and knows God. Anyone who does not love
does not know God, because God is love.*

1 JOHN 4:7–8 ESV

Lord, sometimes I find it difficult to love my fellow humans. They are not always lovely, not always easy to love. They sometimes speak ill of others, skirt the truth, and act selfishly. Yet sometimes I too am guilty of those things. Still, Lord, I know that You love them and me. So, I pray You would send me Your love, the love I need to love others.

It's difficult to fathom that You who are the very essence of love, love me—a woman of so many faults, one who has incurred so many cuts and bruises. But You call me Your beloved because I am precious in Your eyes. Your love has tenderized my heart and opened my mind to loving in return.

Lord, if You can love me with that kind of love, then I can love the unlovely, the unlovable You put on my pathway. Help me to begin loving another today by performing an act of kindness for someone and, in so doing, be a conduit of Your compassionate love and power-filled light. Amen.

Diligent Seekers

*"I love those who love me; and those who seek
me early and diligently will find me."*
PROVERBS 8:17 AMP

Lord, I am so imperfect, so easily swayed. I make so many missteps that I wonder how You, a holy God, can ever love me. But then I read in Your Word that You love those who love You. That the woman who diligently seeks after You will find You.

So I ask You in this moment, Lord, to help me seek You earnestly. To make a good and energetic effort to get closer to You each morning, to learn more of You each day, and to rest in You each evening.

Lord, I must admit that there are times when I'm reading Your Word that I get distracted. I find myself thinking of all the things I have to do. And sometimes when I pray, I fall asleep and simply drift off into never-never land.

So I ask You, Lord, to help me be steady in my pursuit of You. To put all my effort into seeking You in Your Word and through prayer. To help me begin today to get out of my head and into Your spirit and heart. Amen.

He Loves Me

*He placed me at his banquet table, for everyone to
see that his banner over me declares his love. . . . His
left hand cradles my head; his right embraces me.*
SONG OF SOLOMON 2:4, 6 VOICE

. . . .

Dearest Lord, You have stretched a banner over me. And that banner is love. It proclaims that I belong to You, that You love me, that You have always loved me. You love me now and will continue to love me in the future. Even as I sit here, in this moment, focused on You and Your love, I can feel Your left hand cradling my head as Your right hand embraces me.

Knowing this truth keeps me ensconced in Your presence, longing to spend time with You. . .in silence. Knowing that You have declared Your love for me shows me and the world that I belong to You. I am never alone and never will be. You are always with me. Whether I am walking, standing, running, or lying still, I am safely held in Your loving embrace. There, in You, with You, beside You, I can find the strength that I need, the path I am to follow, the love my heart desires. Living in the surety of Your love, all my doubts dissipate. And I am left alone with You. Amen!

See What Kind of Love

See what an incredible quality of love the Father
has shown to us, that we would [be permitted to]
be named and called and counted the children of
God! And so we are! For this reason the world does
not know us, because it did not know Him.

1 JOHN 3:1 AMP

Lord, it's hard enough for me to imagine that You, the God of all gods, Lord of all lords, You whose presence is compared to a strong wind, a hot fire, a strong torrent of water, have called me as Your daughter. Your child.

Although this truth seems incomprehensible, I delight in it. It assuages all my guilt, removes any doubts that may be lingering in the corners of my mind. And it makes me feel special that You called me by my name to come to You and be a member of Your family.

May I rise each morning certain of Your love for me and Your nearness to me. May I walk this earth knowing that because I am Your daughter, I need never fear being separated from You. Instead, as a member of Your family, I who know You and continue to seek Your presence, will be with You forever, loving and being loved. It doesn't get any better than this! Amen.

God's Steadfast Love

But I am like a green olive tree in the house of God.
I trust in the steadfast love of God forever and ever.
PSALM 52:8 ESV

Lord, when I read the psalms, it seems there were times David doubted Your love. He struggled to know that Your loving presence surrounded him at all times. Although he went through some deep, dark times, when he showed his doubts, when he sensed his vulnerability, *even then* You loved him and You protected him. Throughout His life and all through his trials, he grew more and more in tune with Your steadfast love—Your love that is always there, just for the taking.

Lord, teach me what Your steadfast, unfaltering, eternal love is like. When I am going through a difficult time, help me not make it worse by eschewing Your love but instead embracing Your unfaltering love. For then my heart will be lifted up above all my troubles and enjoin with Yours in the kingdom of God. There, above the fray, I will get Your view of the situation, absorb Your wisdom, and be renewed in Your strength.

I thank You, Lord, for Your steadfast love. May I forever trust in it. Amen.

First Loved

We, though, are going to love—love and be loved.
First we were loved, now we love. He loved us first.
1 JOHN 4:19 MSG

Dear Lord, You loved me before the foundation of the world—before You created all that exists. In spite of the missteps You knew I would make, You loved me. You knew there would be times in my life that I would be unfaithful to You or, even worse, refuse to acknowledge You. Yet even then You loved me.

And because You loved me first, Lord, I could not help but love You. For You saw in me what I could not see in myself. You chose me to be Your child, began to mold me into the woman You had created me to be, reached down into my heart and placed Your great love for me there. And I was forever changed.

There's no doubt that Your love enables me to love my fellow humans—even the unlovely.

Lord, thank You for loving me first, for drawing me unto Yourself. Thank You for planting Your love in my heart so that I would love You, others, even myself. Amen.

No Separation

I am convinced that nothing can ever separate
us from God's love. Neither death nor life, neither
angels nor demons, neither our fears for today nor our
worries about tomorrow—not even the powers of hell
can separate us from God's love. No power in the sky
above or in the earth below—indeed, nothing in all
creation will ever be able to separate us from the love
of God that is revealed in Christ Jesus our Lord.
ROMANS 8:38–39 NLT

Lord, when I am filled with doubts about Your love for me, I pray You would quickly come to my rescue and convince me of the truth found in today's verses.

When I feel far away from Your light and touch, Your assurance and comfort, remind me that nothing can ever separate me from the love You hold for me. Nothing in death nor in life, no angel and no demon, not even my fear around what may happen today or my worries about tomorrow have any effect in the free flow of Your love to me.

I pray You would help me and all the others You call, Lord—all the others who have chosen to embark upon Your way—to keep the reality of Your awesome love and its attachment to us in the forefront of our minds as we walk this road with You. Amen.

God's Love Poured into Us

*Hope [in God's promises] never disappoints us, because
God's love has been abundantly poured out within our
hearts through the Holy Spirit who was given to us.*
ROMANS 5:5 AMP

. . . .

Lord, I thank You for Your Holy Spirit who lives within me—to guide me, keep me, teach me, and seal me. You have poured Your love into my heart through that same Spirit—and I am filled to overflowing. In my mind's eye, I see a constant stream of light and warmth coming down upon me, embracing me, enfolding me, penetrating through my skin to the deepest inner recesses of my soul.

Your love compels me to love and minister to others, to see their needs, and respond to them. It is in and on Your love that I rest. That I find my peace. That I find my comfort.

No matter what comes into my life, I can depend on Your love sustaining me, sheltering me, uplifting me, unchaining me. May I be a conduit of that blessing, reaching out to others so that they too may be filled to the utmost with the greatest of Your treasures—Your love. Amen.

Grace, Love, and an Intimate Friend

The amazing grace of the Master, Jesus
Christ, the extravagant love of God, the intimate
friendship of the Holy Spirit, be with all of you.
2 CORINTHIANS 13:14 MSG

Dear Lord, I thank You for the assurance of Your love. Sometimes, when I'm enduring hardship, trials, and troubles, it can be difficult to remember or even believe that Your love is with me. Help me to always remember that Your love is extravagant, which means You have an abundance of it flowing from Your heart into mine as fast as I am able to take it in!

And with that extravagant love comes Jesus' amazing grace. Knowing that He came here to die in my place and to take the punishment that I deserved staggers my mind, reminding me that I can never pay back all that I owe You!

Then, as if Your gift of love and grace were not enough, You blessed me with the constant and continual fellowship of the Holy Spirit. He is my shield and protector, my teacher who will lead me to all truth.

May I never doubt but every day rest in Your gift of amazing grace, extravagant love, and the intimate friendship of Your Holy Spirit. Now and forever. Amen.

A Warrior Who Saves

*"The Lord your God is in your midst, a Warrior who
saves. He will rejoice over you with joy; He will be
quiet in His love [making no mention of your past
sins], He will rejoice over you with shouts of joy."*
ZEPHANIAH 3:17 AMP

When I feel as if I am all alone in this battle, when I doubt that You are near me, when I am burdened by all my missteps, when I feel unworthy of Your love, Lord, remind me of today's verse. Perhaps even plant it in my mind, burn it into my brain, help me always to remember the facts, the truth of my situation.

Your Word tells me that You are always in my midst. Wherever I go, You go. All I need to do is open the eyes of my heart and You will reveal Yourself there. You are not just some wimpy god but *the* God. My warrior. The one who will stand up for me, come between me and my enemies, fight my battles for me.

Not only will You rejoice over me, but You don't revisit all the ways I've disappointed not just myself but You. When my plans go awry, You won't say, "I told you so," but will rush out to meet me, hold me, hug me to Yourself until my tears are dry.

Thank You, Warrior God, for Your unsurpassable love. In Jesus' name, amen.

Guided by Love

The Lord is true to His promises; He will hold you up and
guard you against the evil one. . . . May the Lord guide
your hearts into God's pure love and keep you headed
straight into the strong and sure grip of the Anointed One.
2 THESSALONIANS 3:3, 5 VOICE

. . . .

Dear Jesus, not one of Your promises has ever failed. What You say happens; every word You breathe comes to fruition. So when the evil one sends doubts my way, I pray that You would keep me from drowning in His river of lies. I pray that You would hear my cry and come to my rescue. That You would lift me up from his dark waters and guide my heart back to the clarity of Your light. For there will I find Your true and pure love. There I will find my feet again, be redirected, my course firmly aligned with Your way, the way of the Anointed One, the only one of whose love I am certain. For You, Jesus, are the personification of love, just as the evil one is the personification of lies.

So keep me from going adrift, Lord. Lead me to Your Word and truth each and every day. And if you see me drifting, I pray You, my lifeguard, would come to my aid. Amen.

No Greater Love

"No one has greater love [nor stronger commitment]
than to lay down his own life for his friends."
JOHN 15:13 AMP

Lord, when I think of what You have done for me, how You sent Your Son, Jesus, to save me from the dark, to lift me out of the pit of despair, I am overwhelmed. For it can be nothing other than Your holy, abundant, and compassionate love poured into Him that prompted Him, gave Him the fortitude to keep moving forward—to set His face toward Jerusalem, to the cross, even though You knew the physical pain and mental agony that would entail. Still, Jesus committed Himself to be put in the hands of evil men—and then forgave them as He watched from the cross while His disciples deserted Him.

How You and Your Son can still love humankind is beyond me. But for that love I am now and will forever be eternally grateful. May I never turn back from faithfully following You. May I leave behind all my doubts and misgivings and simply keep my hand in the hand of the Jesus who gave up His life for me and, by doing so, showed the greatest love of all. In His name I pray, amen.

Love Taken Root

If someone responds to and obeys His word, then God's
love has truly taken root and filled him. This is how we
know we are in an intimate relationship with Him.
1 JOHN 2:5 VOICE

. . . .

Lord, when doubts abound about what I'm doing with my life, when I'm unsure about the decisions I'm making, when I no longer have any clue as to what road I'm on, lead me into Your Word. Allow Your voice to move my hands, feet, spirit, and mind to respond to what I'm reading. Prompt Your Word to feed the spirit within me.

Then, Lord, give me the power and wisdom to obey Your Word. For there I will find solid ground. With You walking by my side, I will know which way to go, what to do. With Your love deep in my heart, all my doubts will fade and I will find myself walking Your way with a surer step.

When I'm on Your pathway, Lord, obeying Your will instead of my own, following Your commands instead of society's demands, I will then realize that Your love and peace have finally taken root deep within my soul. That Your peace and calm have overtaken me. Amen.

The Bands of Love

I led them gently with cords of a man, with bonds of
love [guiding them], and I was to them as one who
lifts up and eases the yoke [of the law] over their
jaws; and I bent down to them and fed them.

HOSEA 11:4 AMP

Lord, You led Your chosen people out of Egypt with bonds of love. You led Your children through the wilderness. As any good father would, You provided them with water when they thirsted. You bent down and fed them with meat, then manna, when they hungered. You gently and lovingly cared for them.

When I came to life in faith, You adopted me into Your family. I am now one of Your chosen children. As such, I trust You will lead me through this life with bonds of love.

You have promised to ease my yoke. So I come to You with a heavy burden. I pray You would lighten my load. That You will demonstrate Your love for me, bend down and feed me with the manna of Your Word, that You will quench my thirst with Your living water. Then I will rise strengthened, lifted, assured that You do love me, my burden eased. In Jesus' name, I pray, amen.

Abide in His Love

"I've loved you the way my Father has loved me.
Make yourselves at home in my love. If you keep
my commands, you'll remain intimately at home in
my love. That's what I've done—kept my Father's
commands and made myself at home in his love."
JOHN 15:10 MSG

Jesus, Lord of my heart and life, there are days when I feel anything but loved or lovable. But then I turn to Your Word and read the truth of my situation. Just as Your Father loved You, You love me. That concept is somewhat hard to grasp. But I feel the truth of it deep within.

So here I am, Lord Jesus. I resolve to make myself at home in Your love. To understand that it is there for the taking—anytime, anywhere, any way.

Assured of Your love for me, I find the strength and power I need to follow Your lead. To live as You lived, do as You did, speak as You spoke, love as You loved. So give me Your Word today as well as Your will. Command what You would have me do, and I will obey. For I know You stand by my side, Your love feeding my faith, Your song ringing in my mind. Amen.

Everlasting Love

This is what I, the Eternal One, declare to you: My people who survived the sword found grace as they wandered in the wilderness; when Israel went in search of rest, I appeared to them from far away and said: "I have loved you with an everlasting love—out of faithfulness I have drawn you close."

JEREMIAH 31:3 VOICE

• •

Dear God, when I grow weary and things don't seem to be going my way, doubt slips into my heart. And before I know it, I begin to turn to the world for relief or begin to take things into my own hands. But I know, deep within, that turning myself to the world and following my will is not the way I want to go.

So I pray that You, Lord, would help me get it into my head and heart that You are real, You do love me, and You will never stop loving me. Bring to my mind all the times You have come through for me—answered my prayers beyond what I'd ever hoped or imagined, protected me from seen and unseen evils, brought me out of the darkness and into the light, out of the abyss and into the clouds.

Thank You for loving me no matter how much I wander or wonder. Thank You for blessing me with a forever kind of love. In Jesus' name, amen.

His Love on the Line

We can understand someone dying for a person worth
dying for, and we can understand how someone good
and noble could inspire us to selfless sacrifice. But God
put his love on the line for us by offering his Son in
sacrificial death while we were of no use whatever to him.
ROMANS 5:7–8 MSG

Lord, it is so hard for me to fathom the idea, the *truth* that You sacrificed Your Son on my behalf—on behalf of all believers—when I was of no use to You whatsoever. When I was just a gleam in my father's eye, Your Son, Jesus, died for me. When I was walking in darkness, He died for me. When I was wandering in the wilderness, He died for me.

Your Son put His love on the line for me. And now I hope to live a life worthy of His hope, to walk a way in which He will find some worth.

Thank You, Lord, for saving me and so many others. Help me to remain true to You, to keep up my faith, to love as You loved, to become as selfless as You. May I too put my love on the line and, in so doing, draw others to Your light, life, and love. In Jesus' name, amen.

The God of Love and Peace

Finally, believers, rejoice! Be made complete [be what you
should be], be comforted, be like-minded, live in peace
[enjoy the spiritual well-being experienced by believers
who walk closely with God]; and the God of love and
peace [the source of lovingkindness] will be with you.
2 CORINTHIANS 13:11 AMP

Dear Lord, I am weary of this world's contentiousness, seeking after money, an appetite for power, and disregard for the welfare of others. So I come to You, Lord, looking for love and aid as I walk in this world. I pray that You would help me to become the woman You designed me to be. Lead me to a place of rejoicing as I walk in Your footsteps. Give me comfort when my heart breaks. Help me come to a place of understanding when it comes to working and living beside other believers, so that we may walk in the rhythm of Your will, not our own.

When I do all these things, when I seek You out and allow You to be Lord of my life, when I strive to align myself with You, then and only then am I assured that You, the God of love and peace—the source of all I need, desire, seek, pine for—will be with me. In Jesus' name I pray, amen.

When You Doubt

Your Gifts and Abilities

. . . .

Just as each one of you has received a special gift [a
spiritual talent, an ability graciously given by God],
employ it in serving one another as [is appropriate
for] good stewards of God's multi-faceted grace.

1 PETER 4:10 AMP

We Each Have Different Gifts

In his grace, God has given us different gifts for doing
certain things well. So if God has given you the ability
to prophesy, speak out with as much faith as God has
given you. If your gift is serving others, serve them
well. If you are a teacher, teach well. If your gift is to
encourage others, be encouraging. If it is giving, give
generously. If God has given you leadership ability,
take the responsibility seriously. And if you have a
gift for showing kindness to others, do it gladly.
ROMANS 12:6—8 NLT

Lord, I see others around me working in ministry, using their different gifts in various ways. I see how You have blessed them with their talents. But I'm not sure what my niche may be. Because of this uncertainty, I come to You today and ask You to help me discern what talent You have gifted me with. Reveal to me what ability or skill I can use to serve You, to glorify You. Then I pray that You would give me an outlet in which to use it. For my joy, my desire, my hope is to please You with whatever You have blessed me. In Jesus' name I pray, amen.

Energized by God

There are many different ways to serve, but they're
all directed by the same Lord. There are many
amazing working gifts in the church, but it is the same
God who energizes them all in all who have the gifts.
1 CORINTHIANS 12:5–6 VOICE

Dear Lord, it takes a lot of people serving in many areas to get Your body up and working, sharing Your Word, ministering to others, and spreading Your love and light. And I want to do my part. But I am unsure if I am good enough to do what You are calling me to do. I'm not sure I'm courageous enough, either.

So I come to You today and ask You to assuage my uncertainties, to build up my confidence. Help me to understand that You will give me the power to do whatever You have called me to do. That I do not stand alone when I rise to do Your will.

In the meantime, I realize I may need some practice in honing my talents. At the same time, I don't want my uncertainty to keep me from stepping forward when I am called to move. So I ask You to direct my heart, my talent, my courage, and my strength in regard to what you have gifted me, and help me to use all my talents and energy to Your glory. In Jesus' name, amen.

Stirred Up

This is why I write to remind you to stir up the gift of
God that was conveyed to you when I laid my hands
upon you. You see, God did not give us a cowardly
spirit but a powerful, loving, and disciplined spirit.
2 TIMOTHY 1:6–7 VOICE

- -

Lord, at one time I was given an inkling of the kind of gift You had imparted to me. Then, through prayer and the reading of Your Word, You made clear how You wanted me to serve You.

Yet still I have hesitated to exert myself, to put myself and my gift forward, to do what You have called me to do, use what You have given me in Your name. But You have not gifted me with a spirit that hesitates or fears but one of power, love, and discipline.

So, Lord, help me to dig deep. Help me to understand that You designed me for a purpose, that You have given me a gift to use on this side of heaven. Help me get it clear in my mind that when I came to You, when I welcomed You into my heart, my gift, was awakened and set on a new course. With You, I can boldly do what You would have me do, use what You would have me use, be who You would have me be. Amen.

No Withdrawals

*For the gifts and the calling of God are irrevocable
[for He does not withdraw what He has given, nor
does He change His mind about those to whom He
gives His grace or to whom He sends His call].*

ROMANS 11:29 AMP

. . . .

Lord, I thank You for the gifts You have blessed me with, the calling You have placed upon my heart—and for Your Word that says these gifts and my calling cannot, *will not* be taken back by You. So I ask You, Lord, to open my eyes to whatever dust-laced gifts may be lying around in my spiritual attic, having been left there by me when I lacked the courage to pick them up and give them a go. I pray, Lord, that You would give me the inspiration I need, the strength required to dust them off and see how I might employ them in my service to You.

When You assign me a task, may I consider myself fully able to perform it, to use my gifts in a way that will bring honor and glory to Your name. May You, who've designed me, help me bring my gifts out of the darkness and back into Your light. Amen.

Gifts According as the Spirit Wills

All these things [the gifts, the achievements, the abilities, the empowering] are brought about by one and the same [Holy] Spirit, distributing to each one individually just as He chooses.

1 CORINTHIANS 12:11 AMP

Dear Lord, when I doubt that I am in any way gifted, draw me to the truth of Your Word. May it prompt me to remember that my gifts, the abilities with which You have blessed me, are gifts that may be traced back to the Holy Spirit, *Your* Spirit.

It boggles my mind, Lord, that not only did You call me to be saved and to serve You, but You have prompted Your Spirit to not just bless me with a gift but also empower me to use it. Thank You for choosing me to be a part of Your ministry, to bless others by sharing that with which I have been blessed. Working for You, accomplishing things in Your name—things that please You—is the greatest gift with which You could have ever blessed me.

Today, I seek the power I need to use the abilities You have given me to further Your kingdom, to help bring people into the light. And may all the glory for accomplishing such feats fall to Your credit, Lord. For I am just the instrument You use. In Jesus' name, amen.

Don't Neglect Your Gift

*Teach all these things. And don't let anyone put you
down because you're young. Teach believers with
your life: by word, by demeanor, by love, by faith, by
integrity. Stay at your post reading Scripture, giving
counsel, teaching. And that special gift of ministry you
were given when the leaders of the church laid hands
on you and prayed—keep that dusted off and in use.*
1 TIMOTHY 4:11–14 MSG

Lord, there are times I hesitate to use my gifts. There are others, those who seem to be so much further along on their gift-using journey, and I feel like a youngster just starting out. So I ask You to give me perseverance in honing my gift. Help me dedicate some time each day to the practice of it. And then, Lord, I ask You for the confidence to use it in front of others, to not be dissuaded by whatever comments are made but to focus on working for You while serving others.

Then may I act as an encourager to other people who are bringing their gifts out of their attic for reuse, those continuing to use their gifts over and over again, and those employing their gifts for the first time. May I be their source of encouragement as You are mine. In Jesus' name I pray, amen.

He Gave Gifts to All

Out of the generosity of Christ, each of us is
given his own gift. The text for this is,
He climbed the high mountain,
He captured the enemy and seized the plunder,
He handed it all out in gifts to the people.
EPHESIANS 4:7–8 MSG

Dear Jesus, I stand in awe of what You have done for those who believe in You—given us each our own gift directly from Your hand. Because of Your grace, Your great generosity, You have released us from the power of death and evil. You have sacrificed Your life so that we might have free access to God. In my mind's eye, I can see You climbing the heights, fending off all evil, rising above death, and then seizing the plunder and distributing special gifts to Your people, those who rise up to follow You.

You have made each one of us unique—in size, shape, weight, knowledge, fingerprints, and so on. And to each of us You have given a special gift to use in our own distinctive way. So help me try not to be like someone else or get discouraged because I don't use my gift like someone else does. Instead, Lord, may I be content simply using my talent in whatever way You would have me use it to further Your kingdom of love and light. Amen.

Mutually Encouraged

I long to see you so that I may share with you some
spiritual gift, to strengthen and establish you; that is,
that we may be mutually encouraged and comforted
by each other's faith, both yours and mine.

ROMANS 1:11–12 AMP

Lord, I love today's scripture. For this is a poignant reminder that I am to hone and use my gift, not just to please You or to feel as if I am worthy, but to encourage and uplift those who are in my family of God! This puts a whole new spin on things. It tells me, reminds me, that as I work to please and delight You, I will be pleasing and delighting others.

We all know how it's nice to have one person leading the church singing. But when two or three combine their efforts, they become more engaged in using their talents.

This helps me to realize that I'm wasting my time with a lack of confidence or a perceived idea that I am not good enough to use my abilities to serve You. When I use my gift in conjunction with others, the joy, delight, and pleasure is multiplied!

So show me, Lord, what gifts I can use, where I can use them, and with whom. Let's multiply that joy! Amen.

Alongside

But each has his own gift from God,
one of one kind and one of another.
1 Corinthians 7:7 esv

Thank You, Lord, for giving us each a different kind of gift. If we were all good musicians, who would teach the children? If we were all good at preaching, who would sit in the pews and listen? If we were all good at studying the Word, who would proclaim it?

What's also great is realizing that as long as we do the part God has assigned to us, others will come along and help with the rest. But, like Moses, some of us have such a low opinion of ourselves that we may need You to persuade us to do what You are calling us to do. We may also need someone to come alongside of us to help us with our task, just as You brought Aaron to help Moses, telling the latter, "You shall speak to him and put the words in his mouth, and I will be with your mouth and with his mouth and will teach you both what to do" (Exodus 4:15 esv).

So I praise You, Lord, for the reminder that all I need to do is have the confidence to step out in faith with my gift and You'll provide whoever or whatever is needed to make my efforts shine for Your glory. Amen.

A More Excellent Way

Earnestly desire and strive for the greater gifts [if acquiring them is going to be your goal]. And yet I will show you a still more excellent way [one of the choicest graces and the highest of them all: unselfish love].

1 CORINTHIANS 12:31 AMP

. . . .

Dear Lord, my heart soars with the understanding that all of the gifts we may strive for are nothing if we don't have love, if we don't put others before ourselves. Yet this kind of selflessness is the hardest to attain. We are creatures drawn to seek that which we want, that which we think will make us happy, even though those selfish desires become our downfall.

So here I am, Lord, before You once again, to ask that You help me develop this greatest of graces, this best of ways—unselfish love. Help me not to think of myself first. Help me to be like You and look at what will benefit *all* people, not just me. Help me to not judge others but accept all whose lives touch my own. And may they, in the end, be better for their association with me, not worse.

Lead me into that "more excellent way," Lord, so that I may please You with this greatest of gifts, unselfish love. Amen.

Pursuits

Go after a life of love as if your life depended on it—
because it does. Give yourselves to the gifts God gives you.
1 CORINTHIANS 14:1 MSG

. . . .

I like this idea, Lord, of making love a number one priority in my life. For that's what Your Son did. His priority was to love us above and beyond His own life.

At the same time, Jesus gave Himself to the gifts He had— preaching, teaching, and prophesying. He lived and died pursuing love. And that is the track all His followers are to be on.

So show me, God, how to pursue love like Jesus did. To walk as He walked. At the same time, fuel me with passion so that I can give myself to the gifts You have given me. I like the idea of surrendering myself to whatever talent You would like to come to the fore. I can do that pleasantly, peacefully. *Giving* myself to a gift appeals to me much more than *tackling* one.

Make me a gift, Lord, that will bless others as You have blessed me. In Jesus' name, amen.

For Good

*Use whatever gift you've received for the good of one
another so that you can show yourselves to be good
stewards of God's grace in all its varieties. If you're
called upon to talk, speak as though God put the words
in your mouth; if you're called upon to serve others,
serve as though you had the strength of God behind
you. In these ways, God may be glorified in all you do.*
1 PETER 4:10–11 VOICE

Lord, so many people have so many different gifts. But many falter in
using their gifts because of lack of confidence, strength, energy, power.

Help me, Lord, to turn to You for all I need to use my gift. Remind
me that I'm to do so for Your pleasure and the good of others. If I'm
a speaker, may I speak as though You've given me the words that
need to be said. If I'm a writer, may I write as though You're moving
my pen across the page. If I'm a teacher, may I teach as though
You're giving me the lessons that need to be taught and the energy
to deliver them. If I'm called to sing, may I do so with the belief that
You've not only chosen the song to be sung but are giving me the
power within to sing it.

In all ways, Lord, may I simply be a conduit of Your love and
desire as I use my gifts to Your glory. Amen.

Gifts of the Holy Spirit

When the church in Jerusalem got wind of this, they sent Barnabas to Antioch to check on things. As soon as he arrived, he saw that God was behind and in it all. He threw himself in with them, got behind them, urging them to stay with it the rest of their lives. He was a good man that way, enthusiastic and confident in the Holy Spirit's ways. The community grew large and strong in the Master.

ACTS 11:22–24 MSG

Lord, today's passage is a good reminder that we're to be rolling up our sleeves and using our talents and abilities in areas where we already see You working!

That's what the believer named Barnabas did. In Acts 4:36 (AMP), we read that a man named Joseph, a Levite and a native of Cyprus, was "surnamed Barnabas by the apostles (which translated means Son of Encouragement)." Yet Barnabas went beyond mere encouragement. He dove into helping the believers, doing whatever he could, all the while urging them not to stop, to never give up their work.

I pray, Lord, that You would give me eyes to see where You are working. Then give me the confidence and enthusiasm to use my gifts to encourage and help others. Amen.

Right Alongside

Just think—you don't need a thing, you've got it
all! All God's gifts are right in front of you as you
wait expectantly for our Master Jesus to arrive on
the scene for the Finale. And not only that, but God
himself is right alongside to keep you steady and on
track until things are all wrapped up by Jesus. God,
who got you started in this spiritual adventure, shares
with us the life of his Son and our Master Jesus.
He will never give up on you. Never forget that.
1 CORINTHIANS 1:7–9 MSG

Lord, Your Word makes it clear I lack nothing—not even a spiritual gift. Because all of the gifts You meant for me are here in front of me! All I need to do is unwrap them. You'll help me learn to use what You have gifted me, working right alongside of me! That idea is so empowering, supplanting my doubts and increasing my confidence. For I know that with You, nothing is impossible!

So continue to keep me on track, Lord. Help me to understand that someday Jesus will return, but I need not keep looking over my shoulder. Instead, may You find me diligently serving You when He comes back.

I thank You, Lord, for sharing the life—and death—of Your Son with me. Knowing You will never give up on me makes it a whole lot easier to continue this fantastic adventure. In Jesus' name, amen.

If I Don't Love

*If I speak with human eloquence and angelic ecstasy
but don't love, I'm nothing but the creaking of a rusty
gate. If I speak God's Word with power, revealing
all his mysteries and making everything plain as
day, and if I have faith that says to a mountain,
"Jump," and it jumps, but I don't love, I'm nothing.*
1 CORINTHIANS 13:1–2 MSG

Lord, in Your Word, You go to great lengths to make it clear that without love, I am nothing. That if in all I do and say—writing, speaking, teaching, mentoring, singing, repairing, building, preaching—if I don't love, I'm nothing. In other words, without love, it doesn't matter what talents I use or the amount of confidence I have in using them. It will all be for and come to naught if I don't have love.

So I pray, Lord, that You help me etch this idea firmly on the surface of my mind. Help me to understand that if I am to do what You call me to do, if I am to use the gifts You have put before me, I am to first and foremost do so in and with love. For You *are* love. Amen.

Three Magic Words

*"Come, I will send you to Pharaoh that you may bring
my people, the children of Israel, out of Egypt." But
Moses said to God, "Who am I that I should go to
Pharaoh and bring the children of Israel out of Egypt?"*
EXODUS 3:10–11 ESV

Lord, sometimes when You are calling me to a task, I wonder how I can do it. I doubt that I am equipped—with the talent and courage—to do what You're asking.

It seems I'm not alone. Even Moses did not feel qualified to bring the children of Israel out of Egypt. Yet, when he presented his doubts to You, You said those five magical words: "I will be with you" (Exodus 3:12 ESV).

You knew Moses could accomplish what You were requesting him to do. And, in the same way, You know what I can do. You have gifted me with particular talents and abilities so that I can perform that which You have designed me to perform. All I need to remember is that You, the God of all, are with me—helping me, leading me, empowering me, standing alongside of me.

Thank You, Lord, for the assurance of Your Word and of Your presence. For I know that with You, I can do anything. In Jesus' name, amen.

Every Good Gift

*Every good thing given and every perfect gift is from
above; it comes down from the Father of lights [the
Creator and Sustainer of the heavens], in whom there
is no variation [no rising or setting] or shadow cast by
His turning [for He is perfect and never changes].*
JAMES 1:17 AMP

Lord, when I am full of doubts, unsure how to use my abilities and my talents to further Your kingdom, remind me that You know exactly what I am, who I am, how I am fashioned, and what I am fashioned for, because You have done the fashioning.

Although my parents may have had some hand in molding me, in shaping me in this world and preparing me for it, You, Lord, are the source of my gifts—talents exactly suited to me and to be used for You.

So I pray that You would fill me, Lord, with a spirit of confidence. Make it clear to me the gifts with which You have blessed me. Then help me to hone my abilities. Show me how and where You would have me use them for ministry. And in doing so, may I in all ways, bring honor to You. In Jesus' name I pray, amen.

According to Ability

*"For it is just like a man who was about to take a journey,
and he called his servants together and entrusted them
with his possessions. To one he gave five talents, to
another, two, and to another, one, each according to
his own ability; and then he went on his journey."*
MATTHEW 25:14–15 AMP

Lord, You have allocated talents to me. And in Your wisdom, You have given me only what I'm able to manage in accordance with my abilities, which also come from Your good hand.

So gone are the notions that I am not up for the job. Gone is the false idea that I'm overtaxed, unable to handle all You have blessed me with.

Today I am here to ask You to be very present in my life. To remind me that regardless of my age, gender, and status, I can learn; I can grow; I can practice, exercise, and make good on whatever opportunities You afford me. I am and always will be useful to You.

No matter how others see me—as simply a wife, a mother, a believer, a sister, a daughter, a friend—You see me as a gifted person, a strong woman who serves You. Help me do that each day, Lord. Help me rest in the confidence that You will never give me more than I can handle but will, instead, make the most of what I give You. Amen.

Hidden Talent

"The servant given one thousand said, 'Master, I know
you have high standards and hate careless ways,
that you demand the best and make no allowances
for error. I was afraid I might disappoint you, so I
found a good hiding place and secured your money.
Here it is, safe and sound down to the last cent.'"

MATTHEW 25:25 MSG

. . . .

Oh Lord, may I not allow fear to keep me from using the talents You have given me. May I not allow my feelings of inadequacy to prevent me from doing the most I can with what You have blessed me with. May I not let my lack of confidence so overwhelm me that I hide my talents from Your eyes, my eyes, and the eyes of the world.

Help me not to wallow in doubt, allowing the fears of disappointing You or embarrassing myself rule over me. Instead, give me the strength and determination, the confidence and assurance to rise up, to break through any self- or world-imposed barriers to do the best with which You have gifted me. For I long to sing for You, play for You, preach and teach for You, to lead for You, to serve You in whatever ways You direct me. Amen.

Out on a Limb

*"The master was furious. 'That's a terrible way to
live! It's criminal to live cautiously like that! If you
knew I was after the best, why did you do less than
the least? The least you could have done would have
been to invest the sum with the bankers, where at
least I would have gotten a little interest. Take the
thousand and give it to the one who risked the most.
And get rid of this "play-it-safe" who won't go out
on a limb. Throw him out into utter darkness.'"*
MATTHEW 25:26–30 MSG

Dear Lord, the only way to live this life is to dedicate myself to You
with abandon. To use my gifts and talents in whichever way You
please, whenever and wherever You please. To not allow my fears
and misgivings, my lack of confidence and doubts, to keep me from
doing exactly what You have equipped me and asked me to do.

My sole desire is to follow where You lead. To take Your words
as my gospel. To trust that You know what is best for me in this life.
To go out on a limb, to take a chance. For I want to hear You say,
"Well done, good and faithful servant. Good work, My daughter. You
have done well. Come, share in My joy. Come, and be My partner."

In Jesus' name I trust and pray, amen.

The Search

"Ask and keep on asking and it will be given to you; seek and keep on seeking and you will find; knock and keep on knocking and the door will be opened to you. For everyone who keeps on asking receives, and he who keeps on seeking finds, and to him who keeps on knocking, it will be opened."
MATTHEW 7:7–8 AMP

Lord, some of my gifts may change over the years. What I was able to do in my younger days may seem more difficult in my more mature years. So here I am, at this point in my life, coming before You, asking You to make plain what You would have me do.

I apply to You, Lord, the source of my gifts, abilities, life, and breath. Make it clear what You would have me do at this juncture in my life. Help me as I seek the confidence to do what You require. And show me the doors of opportunity You would have me knock on. Lead me to where You would have me go and what You would have me do when I get there.

If, Lord, this asking, seeking, and knocking are to be done slowly—if my gifts are to be explored, then used in stages—I ask You to be by my side as I take this journey. Help me to yield myself and my abilities to You. And lastly, give me the confidence to see things through. Amen.

Rich in Acts

Now in Joppa there was a disciple named Tabitha, (which translated into Greek means Dorcas). She was rich in acts of kindness and charity which she continually did.
ACTS 9:36 AMP

As I seek to discover what abilities You have given me, Lord, help me not to disregard the gifts that may seem insignificant in the eyes of others. If You have given me a talent that will help those who are poor in wealth or spirit, may I make the most of it.

No matter what my specialty is, may I, like Your servant Dorcas, be "rich in acts of kindness and charity." And may I be consistent in the same.

May the love You have blessed me with give me the courage and inspiration to love and serve those who may be less fortunate. May I use my hands and my feet in whatever way You call me to use them—whether to help my fellow believers or to reach out to those who are poor, widowed, or downtrodden. May I do so with the confidence that You will continually supply me with not only the talent I need to serve but with the time and finances that may be required. Amen.

Serving in Love

It is absolutely clear that God has called you to a free life. Just make sure that you don't use this freedom as an excuse to do whatever you want to do and destroy your freedom. Rather, use your freedom to serve one another in love; that's how freedom grows. For everything we know about God's Word is summed up in a single sentence: Love others as you love yourself. That's an act of true freedom.
GALATIANS 5:13–14 MSG

Lord, You have blessed me with the freedom to serve You and others in love. So I pray that I would never use that God-given freedom to satisfy my own desires or ego but to serve others—and to do so in love. Just like Mary, who broke that expensive bottle of perfume with which she anointed Your feet, then sat listening to every word that dropped from Your mouth, loving You with her attention, her acts, her awe.

You, Lord, are the personification of love. So I pray that I would be ever mindful of Your presence within me. Keep me cognizant of the fact that I am not to exercise my gifts so that I will receive the accolades but so that others would be drawn to You, Your love, Your light, Your Word. Amen.

Get Up and Go

Now in Damascus there was a disciple named Ananias;
and the Lord said to him in a vision, "Ananias." And
he answered, "Here I am, Lord." And the Lord said
to him, "Get up and go to the street called Straight,
and ask at the house of Judas for a man from
Tarsus named Saul; for he is praying [there]."
ACTS 9:10–11 AMP

Lord, I may have willingly answered Your call. I may be open to Your voice, direction, guidance. But I must admit that, at times, my doubts and fears around using them keep me from following Your commands.

Ananias had the same misgivings when You asked him to seek out Saul from Tarsus, to place his hands on Saul, to pray over him so that he could regain his sight. Ananias had already heard about Saul, "about the terrible things this man has done to the believers in Jerusalem! And he is authorized by the leading priests to arrest everyone who calls upon your name" (Acts 9:13–14 NLT). But then, after You told Ananias to go anyway, that Paul was to become Your mouthpiece to Gentiles and kings, he obeyed without further question.

May I too, Lord, be Your willing servant, one whose hesitation You will overcome, one who will willingly, courageously, faithfully, and obediently use her gifts at Your request. Amen.

A Willing Body

On the way to the place of crucifixion, they pulled a
man from the crowd—his name was Simon of Cyrene,
a person from the countryside who happened to be
entering the city at that moment. They put Jesus' cross
on Simon's shoulders, and he followed behind Jesus.
LUKE 23:26 VOICE

Lord Jesus, I remember well the story of Your crucifixion. How Simon of Cyrene, a man who'd just happened to be coming into the city when You walked by, was made to help carry the heavy bar for Your cross. He was just a body that showed up at the right time and right place. How blessed he must have felt when he realized who You were and what was happening.

I too want to be there for You, Lord. A willing body, an obedient servant, ready to do what You need done. For whether I serve You with my gifts or simply with my hands, I am here for You—and whoever else You put into my life.

So here I am, Lord. Whatever my gifts, whatever my strength, whatever You need, I am Your obedient servant to use in whatever way You desire. Employ me as You see fit. And I will serve as I am ready, willing, and able. Amen.

Working Up Courage

*Joseph of Arimathea, a highly respected member of the
Jewish Council, came. He was one who lived expectantly,
on the lookout for the kingdom of God. Working up his
courage, he went to Pilate and asked for Jesus' body.*

MARK 15:43 MSG

Lord Jesus, I hold Joseph of Arimathea in admiration. Although he
kept his belief in You a secret, he did manage to work up his courage
and do the right thing in the end. But he didn't stop there. After he
retrieved Your body, he bought a linen shroud, wrapped You in it, and
placed You in his very own tomb, rolling a rock before the entrance.
What courage! What a sacrifice!

Your Word reminds Your servants that we may obtain boldness
and access our confidence through our faith in You (Ephesians 3:12).
Make me that bold, Lord. Give me the confidence I need to do the
right thing by You and for others.

Pour upon me a good dose of courage, Lord. For I long to heed
Your call to serve, love, and do for You. Not just today. And not just
tomorrow. But now and always. In Your name I pray, amen.

When You Doubt

Your Faith

. . . .

*Trust in the LORD with all your heart, and do not
lean on your own understanding. In all
your ways acknowledge him, and he
will make straight your paths.*
PROVERBS 3:5–6 ESV

Little Faith

*Jesus immediately reached out his hand and took
hold of him, saying to him, "O you of little faith,
why did you doubt?" And when they got into
the boat, the wind ceased. And those in the boat
worshiped him, saying, "Truly you are the Son of God."*
MATTHEW 14:31–33 ESV

Dear Lord, I must admit there are times when I am somewhat like Peter: of little faith. Instead of keeping my eyes on You, my focus tends to wander. Instead of looking to You, the Son of God, the calmer of chaos and cooler of calamity, I become fixated on the wind and water. And the next thing I know, I begin sinking beneath the waves.

Help me, Lord, to build up my belief. Keep me from faltering in my faith. Remind me that You are in control of all my surroundings, all my problems, all my fears. That You will calm all the storms in my life.

Oh Lord, when I feel the weakest, when the turbulence of this life threatens to overwhelm me, and I cry out to You, increase my faith that I might be a testimony of You, Your might, and Your power. For when my faith is strong, I can walk on water. Amen.

Response to Faith

*They brought to Him a man who was paralyzed, lying
on a stretcher. Seeing their [active] faith [springing
from confidence in Him], Jesus said to the paralytic,
"Do not be afraid, son; your sins are forgiven [the
penalty is paid, the guilt removed, and you are
declared to be in right standing with God]."*
MATTHEW 9:2 AMP

Dear Lord, I long to have my faith be as strong as the friends of the paralytic, a faith so great that You can see it, hear it, feel it in the air.

Too often I am overwhelmed by doubt. Too often, I trust in my own strength and ability, thinking I can solve the problems that face me. Yet it is in You alone I must trust. For when I do, I find myself blessed with the peace that comes with knowing *You* are in control, not I. Admitting that I don't have all the answers, that I can't fix every problem, relieves my stress and frustration a thousandfold.

Help me build up my faith, Lord. Give me the intelligence to turn all things—including myself—over to You. For it is You alone who has control over all that is seen and all that is unseen.

May I one day have a visible faith, one that prompts You to say, "Do not be afraid, daughter. All is well." Amen.

Have Faith in God

*Jesus replied, "Have faith in God [constantly]. I assure
you and most solemnly say to you, whoever says to this
mountain, 'Be lifted up and thrown into the sea!' and
does not doubt in his heart [in God's unlimited power],
but believes that what he says is going to take place, it
will be done for him [in accordance with God's will]."*
MARK 11:22–23 AMP

Lord, I'm tired of finding myself entertaining my doubts, letting my worries control my life. The load of this world is way too much for me to handle. So I come with my faith in hand and mind, seeking Your face, Your wisdom, Your will.

If my desire aligns with Yours, I pray, Lord, that You will lift up all those challenges, worries, and doubts that are plaguing my mind as You would a mountain. And in Your great and unlimited power, I pray You would toss that mountain into the sea and allow it to sink under the surface of the waters.

It is this faith in You that will strip me of all needless concerns and worries and make me a more fit woman—ready, willing, and able to serve You. In Jesus' name I pray, amen.

Saving Faith

Jesus said to the woman, "Your faith [in Me] has saved you; go in peace [free from the distress experienced because of sin]."

LUKE 7:50 AMP

Lord, what a level of faith this woman had for You. For she went in—as sinful as she was—with nothing but love in her heart and complete trust in Your accepting and returning her love. That's the kind of faith I long to possess.

So here I am before You, Lord. My entire being—mind, body, heart, spirit, and soul—bows to You in love. Dripping with trust, knowing You will accept me as I am, I take this time, this moment, and pour my love upon You like a flowing fountain of perfume. Regardless of the time, money, and effort this takes from me, I love You willingly and enthusiastically. As I do so, I discover the amazing peace that comes upon me, being here in Your presence, knowing that You take me—and love me—as I am. Basking in Your acceptance of me, Your compassion for me, and Your forgiveness of me, my heart is overwhelmed. And by Your words, I find my saving faith and my peace. Amen.

Testing, Testing

In this you rejoice, though now for a little while,
if necessary, you have been grieved by various
trials, so that the tested genuineness of your faith—
more precious than gold that perishes though it is
tested by fire—may be found to result in praise and
glory and honor at the revelation of Jesus Christ.

1 PETER 1:6–7 ESV

. . . .

Dear Lord, when I am being tested, I want to cry out for deliverance. I want my situation to disappear. I want a stop to the pain, the worry, and the doubt that threaten to overwhelm me.

When stress and frustration begin, I turn from You and Your Word, tapping into my human wisdom, looking to do what I can to turn my situation around.

But I inevitably find myself spinning my wheels—because I can do nothing without You. I cannot save myself. When I've come to the end of myself, the Holy Spirit scatters a shaft of Son-light upon me, nudging me back to You. Soon I find myself back in Your Word. There I find Your purpose in the testing. There I pray that I will come out of this experience with a more real faith, one that looks to You for help, harbor, and healing. One that never fails to deliver on peace. In Jesus' name, amen.

A Fashioned Faith

*Faith is the assurance of things you have hoped for,
the absolute conviction that there are realities you've
never seen. It was by faith that our forebears were
approved. Through faith we understand that the
universe was created by the word of God; everything we
now see was fashioned from that which is invisible.*
HEBREWS 11:1–3 VOICE

Although others may scoff, I know that there are realities we cannot see with our naked eyes. That instinct is borne of my faith, Lord. And it is by that faith that I view this world, seeing it as the masterpiece created by You, by Your Word. It was You alone whose spirit-wind hovered over dark, formless, and chaotic water and whose voice brought light, shape, and order to it. You are the one, Lord, who spoke all things into being, making all that was once invisible visible.

I pray that You would speak into my life now, Lord. Hover over me with Your Spirit. Use Your Word to form, shape, and fill me. Bring peace and hope to my life, my heart, my mind. Transform me, who was once invisible to the naked eye, into a being of light—soft yet strong, small yet mighty, weak yet determined to become the woman You designed me to be—for Your name and by Your power. Amen.

Possessed of Faith

By faith Abraham, when he was called [by God], obeyed
by going to a place which he was to receive as an
inheritance; and he went, not knowing where he was
going. . . . By faith even Sarah herself received the ability
to conceive [a child], even [when she was long] past the
normal age for it, because she considered Him who had
given her the promise to be reliable and true [to His word].
HEBREWS 11:8, 11 AMP

Lord, I want to step out in faith possessing the assurance that Abraham had. When You call me, I pray my ears open to Your voice and my will becomes obedient to Your direction. I long to have the faith that will help me walk down the path to which You have called me—even though I may not know exactly where I'm going or what I may possess when I get there.

God of the living and the dead, I want to possess the faith Sarah had. Even though I may not now seem to be a candidate fit for whatever miracle You have in mind, I want to walk with the assurance that You will stay true to Your Word, that You will make good on Your promises, that whatever I desire that is aligned with You will become a reality. Amen.

A Turning of the Mind

"So don't worry about these things, saying, 'What will we eat? What will we drink? What will we wear?' These things dominate the thoughts of unbelievers, but your heavenly Father already knows all your needs. Seek the Kingdom of God above all else, and live righteously, and he will give you everything you need."
MATTHEW 6:31–33 NLT

Heavenly Father, I must admit there are times when my faith seems so miniscule, so pitiful. I am so very concerned about the future, my finances, my family, my welfare. But You tell me not to worry about such things. Why? Because You already know exactly what I need and how and when to provide it.

Thus, Lord, I'm heading on a new course. Instead of allowing my thoughts to careen out of control, instead of being fixated on the what-ifs of life, I'm going to lean on You, to trust You to help me and those I love through this life on earth. I am going to forget about my worries and turn my mind and heart to You and Your Word, seeking You and Your kingdom above all other things. I am going to trust You to provide for and fulfill all my needs. In Jesus' name, amen.

A Sudden Calm

A fierce storm struck the lake, with waves breaking into the boat. But Jesus was sleeping. The disciples went and woke him up, shouting, "Lord, save us! We're going to drown!" Jesus responded, "Why are you afraid? You have so little faith!" Then he got up and rebuked the wind and waves, and suddenly there was a great calm.
MATTHEW 8:24–26 NLT

Lord, there are so many things I'm afraid of, so many things that can rock my boat.

When my life is beleaguered by storms of various shapes and sizes, some of which are of my own making, I'm afraid my life will capsize under the turbulence or break up upon the rocks. I'm so worked up about the latest storm in my life that I find myself nauseous with anxiety.

I ask You, Lord, for more faith. For a stronger trust in You. May I remember that You do care about me. That You aren't sleeping on the job but are riding out the storm with me. Keep me cognizant of the fact that You will take care of me even in the midst of a storm. And that just when the waves seem as if they're at their peak and threaten to pull me under, You will rise up, rebuke the storm swirling around me, and bless me with a great calm. In Jesus' name I pray, amen.

Where Is Your Faith

Then he said to his disciples, "Why can't you trust me?"
They were in absolute awe, staggered and stammering,
"Who is this, anyway? He calls out to the winds and
sea, and they do what he tells them!" They sailed on.
LUKE 8:25–26 MSG

Lord, when I feel tossed and turned by the storms in my life, when things don't go the way I wanted or expected them to, I begin to doubt my trust in You.

Yet You, Lord, have shown that You command even winds and water. Remind me of that fact each and every day. Remind me that the world was created through You, that You are the Lord of the wind, the waves, the weather. Remind me that all I have to do is call out to You, and You will come to my rescue, pull me out of the turbulent tide, and bring me to where You would have me be.

You, Lord, Creator and Sustainer, have promised never to leave me. You have promised not to give me more than I can bear. When things get tough, You have prepared a way of escape for me. For all these things, I thank You. With all my heart, I trust You. You alone can calm the storms—within and without—allowing me to weather all, then sail on. Amen.

Nothing Impossible

"Nothing, you see, is impossible with God."
And Mary said, Yes, I see it all now: I'm the
Lord's maid, ready to serve. Let it be with me
just as you say. Then the angel left her.
LUKE 1:36–38 MSG

Lord, I cannot imagine being visited by an angel as a young girl. But that's what happened with Mary. And when the angel forecast to her what would be happening in her life and divulged what had already happened in the life of her cousin Elizabeth, he reminded her that nothing was impossible with God.

Out of her gentle yet deep faith, Mary accepted the angel's somewhat fantastical prophecy, aligned her will with what was to happen, and admitted she was ready to do whatever God called her to do. She became a ready participant in Your great plan to save Your children.

That's the kind of faith I want, Lord. Sometimes I read Your promises and cannot imagine how You will make them come to pass. But that's not for me to figure out. For You have a way of doing things beyond our finite imaginations. So may I, Lord, remind myself every day that nothing is impossible when You are on the scene. I pray You would open my eyes to possibilities I'd never imagined.

I am ready to serve You, Lord, allowing things to be with me exactly as You say. In Jesus' name, amen.

God's Power

The sermons I preached were not delivered with the
kind of persuasive elegance some have come to
expect, but they were effective because I relied
on God's Spirit to demonstrate God's power. If
this were not so, your faith would be based on
human wisdom and not the power of God.
1 CORINTHIANS 2:4–5 VOICE

So many times, Lord, my lack of faith keeps me from allowing Your power to shine through. When that happens, I end up doing things in my own strength and according to my own wisdom. Living and witnessing in such a way puts the focus on human wisdom and effort, not on Your power.

Help me, Lord, to be a conduit of Your strength in every aspect of my life. To not worry about how things will turn out but to rely on Your Spirit to work through me, to do what needs to be done, to get the message across whether it is written, spoken, or simply felt. May everyone who looks at me see Your Spirit, Your light and wisdom, Your strength and power, Your knowledge and love shining through. For then they will be drawn to You, their faith will blossom under Your hand, and they will find the signposts that You have waiting for them. And all glory will go to You. In Jesus' name, amen.

Just Say the Word

When they approached the Centurion's
home, the Centurion sent out some friends
to bring a message to Jesus.

Message of the Centurion: *Lord, don't go*
to the trouble of coming inside. I am not worthy
to have You come under my roof. That's why I
sent others with my request. Just say the word,
and that will be enough to heal my servant.

LUKE 7:6–7 VOICE

Lord, You are the master of long-distance miracles. Your Word and hands hold such power. All one needs is a touch from You or a word spoken however far away, and her world is changed, her prayers answered.

Help me, Lord, to embed these truths deep in my heart and mind. Help me to understand that You need not have the name or location of the person who needs help nor be in that person's presence. All that is needed is someone—a faith-filled believer—to intercede on behalf of another. And all You need to do is simply say the word, and lives will be changed.

God, make me that faith-filled believer. Help me to have the confidence I need to bring others to You in prayer and believe that You can and will help them—no matter who they are or what they've done. For You are a God of power, compassion, and love. Amen.

If You Have Faith

*"I assure you and most solemnly say to you, if you have
faith [personal trust and confidence in Me] and do not
doubt or allow yourself to be drawn in two directions. . .
if you say to this mountain, 'Be taken up and thrown into
the sea,' it will happen [if God wills it]. And whatever
you ask for in prayer, believing, you will receive."*
MATTHEW 21:21–22 AMP

Lord, when difficulties occur in my life, You are often the last person I go to for help. First, I try to solve my problems on my own. Then, once exhaustion and frustration have taken their toll, then and only then do I come to You.

Help me, Lord, to grow so close to You and so dependent upon You that I trust You with anything and everything. May I be so confident that You are with me, listening to me, witnessing what is happening in my life, that I run to You before making any efforts to "fix" anything. I pray that I would get into the habit of coming to You before I open my mouth, take any action, or expend energy in overthinking the situation.

May I become a woman who is fully reliant upon You, ready to align her will with Yours. May my faith grow to the point that I become certain that whatever I ask for in prayer, I will receive it. Amen (so be it!).

As Smooth as Glass

Awake now, he told the wind to pipe down and
said to the sea, "Quiet! Settle down!" The wind
ran out of breath; the sea became smooth as glass.
Jesus reprimanded the disciples: "Why are you
such cowards? Don't you have any faith at all?"
MARK 4:39–40 MSG

. . . .

Dear Lord, when trouble comes, I find myself riding high on fear and watching my faith go out the window. I know this has to change. When calamity strikes, I want to trust You alone.

Lord, when fear threatens to overwhelm me, display Your mighty power. I know that You are master over all things—natural and unnatural, visible and invisible. I know You can calm the storms of my life.

Remind me that when I put my trust in You, not only does my fear dissipate, but I become calm, unruffled. For I know that with me, holding my hand, keeping me safe, sheltering me above, below, and on all sides, is the all-powerful Lord of lords.

Help me each day, Lord, to get stronger and stronger, calmer and calmer, trusting You more and more until I am firmly convinced and content that You are always with me and will never leave me. Amen.

Wisdom for the Journey

*If you don't have all the wisdom needed for this
journey, then all you have to do is ask God for it; and
God will grant all that you need. He gives lavishly and
never scolds you for asking. The key is that your request
be anchored by your single-minded commitment to God.
Those who depend only on their own judgment are like
those lost on the seas, carried away by any wave or
picked up by any wind. Those adrift on their own wisdom
shouldn't assume the Lord will rescue them or bring
them anything. The splinter of divided loyalty shatters
your compass and leaves you dizzy and confused.*
JAMES 1:5–8 VOICE

. . . .

Father God, too often I find my faith faltering because I'm relying
on my own solutions to problems, answers to questions, wisdom for
the journey. And when I do so, I inevitably find myself stuck or in
trouble, crying out for Your strength and power to lift me out of the
mess I have created.

So I ask You, Lord, to help me make You my sole fount of wisdom.
I do so with the understanding that when You bless me with direction, I will not leave that path once I have embarked upon it. All I
ask, Lord, is that You give me the faith as I pray for Your guidance.
Help me never to waver from the course You set before me. In Jesus'
name and power I pray, amen.

My Champion

Let us strip off every weight that slows us down, especially
the sin that so easily trips us up. And let us run with
endurance the race God has set before us. We do this by
keeping our eyes on Jesus, the champion who initiates
and perfects our faith. Because of the joy awaiting him,
he endured the cross, disregarding its shame. Now he
is seated in the place of honor beside God's throne.
HEBREWS 12:1–2 NLT

Lord, sometimes I feel like I'm spinning my wheels when it comes to my walk of faith. It seems I'm getting nowhere fast. But that's all on me, Lord. I'm clinging to disappointments, unforgiveness, mistakes, and bitterness. No wonder I'm frustrated and exhausted.

So here I am, praying that You will help me shrug off all that's holding me back, tripping me up. With eyes wide open and my mind clear, I'm running to You, Jesus—You, my champion, the one who designed my faith and will get me to the finish line. You who sit on the throne beside God have all my attention. To You I pray I will one day say, "I have fought the good fight, I have finished the race, I have kept the faith" (2 Timothy 4:7 ESV).

With that goal in mind, in this moment I ask You, Lord, where shall we start today? What would You have me do? In what area may I grow my faith? Amen.

Conquering Power

The proof that we love God comes when we keep his
commandments and they are not at all troublesome.
Every God-born person conquers the world's ways. The
conquering power that brings the world to its knees is our
faith. The person who wins out over the world's ways is
simply the one who believes Jesus is the Son of God.

1 JOHN 5:2–5 MSG

Father God, when doubts begin to enter my mind, testing and at times obliterating my faith, remind me that my strength lies in keeping Your commandments. Help me get back on track by loving You; seeking You with all my heart, soul, mind, and strength; and by loving myself, the inroad that helps me find the pathway to loving others.

Your commands to love, Lord, always lead me back to You—the God who is love. And when I am close to You, doing as You command, my faith rises up and brings the world to its knees.

Thank You for the love that fuels my faith and wins over the ways of this world. Thank You, Lord, for allowing Your love to work in me and stream through me, spilling out into a world so bereft of love. In Jesus' name I pray, amen.

Strengthened in Faith

David and his men burst out in loud wails—wept and wept until they were exhausted with weeping. David's two wives. . .had been taken prisoner along with the rest. And suddenly David was in even worse trouble. There was talk among the men, bitter over the loss of their families, of stoning him. David strengthened himself with trust in his GOD. He ordered Abiathar the priest, son of Ahimelech, "Bring me the Ephod so I can consult God."
1 SAMUEL 30:5–7 MSG

. . . .

Dear Lord, suffering a loss has a way of pushing my faith away, making me forget who You are and who I am in You. When I am lost in tears and extreme grief, my thoughts go helter-skelter. Then, before I know it, I'm thinking nasty thoughts, looking to blame someone, giving in to my anger and feeling of helplessness.

Yet amid loss and grief is when I should be turning to You, trusting in You, looking to You. For in You I find a balm of strength, faith, hope, and guidance.

So help me, Lord, to allow grief and emotions in but not to let them or my doubts about Your goodness derail my faith. Instead, may I find my footing and my strength within my faith. May I consult You for the best tack to take, then go where You lead, knowing that in You all is made right. Amen.

Confident Trust

*Throwing his cloak aside, he jumped up and came to
Jesus. And Jesus said, "What do you want Me to do for
you?" The blind man said to Him, "Rabboni (my Master),
let me regain my sight." Jesus said to him, "Go; your faith
[and confident trust in My power] has made you well."*

MARK 10:50–52 AMP

Lord, may I, like the blind beggar Bartimaeus, sit by the roadside and, when I hear You coming, shout out for Your mercy. May I not allow others to silence my pleas but continue knocking on Your door until You open it.

When You bid me come, Lord, may I strip off anything that hinders —my ego, my doubts, my fears, my desires—my flight to Your side. And when You ask what I would have You do for me, Lord, may I ask in confidence for the eyes to see You, the ears to hear You, the intelligence to discern You, the wisdom to understand You, and the faith to follow You. May I, Your daughter, hear You say those precious words: "Go; your faith and confident trust in My Words, My ways, My power have made you the woman I created you to be—now and forever." In Jesus' wonderful name and power I pray, amen.

The Lord Stands with Me

At my first defense no one came to stand by me,
but all deserted me. May it not be charged against
them! But the Lord stood by me and strengthened
me. . . . So I was rescued from the lion's mouth.
The Lord will rescue me from every evil deed and
bring me safely into his heavenly kingdom.
2 TIMOTHY 4:16–18 ESV

Lord, when I feel all alone, when it looks as if all have deserted me, may I forgive them. At the same time, may my faith increase all the more as I consider that even with no man or woman to stand beside me, You will never desert me. You will never leave me. You will never abandon me. Instead, may I feel Your presence right beside me, strengthening, helping me to stand, filling me with the courage I need to face the lions roaring against me.

As my good Shepherd, I know You will always be there to protect Your flock. Your Word says, "He will gather together His lambs—the weak and the wobbly ones—into His arms. He will carry them close to His bosom, and tenderly lead like a shepherd the mother of her lambs" (Isaiah 40:11 VOICE). In Your Word, I have hope. In Your presence, I stand. Amen.

Faith over Fear

By faith Moses, after his birth, was hidden for three months by his parents, because they saw he was a beautiful and divinely favored child; and they were not afraid of the king's (Pharaoh's) decree.
HEBREWS 11:23 AMP

When everything seems against me, Lord, when that which I cherish must be turned over to You, set upon the stream of Your will and way, I pray You would give me the strength, faith, and courage to ignore the threats of others and my own inner doubts. Help me put all I love in Your caring and capable hands, then leave the results to You.

As I embark upon this journey of faith, Lord, I realize that fear must be left behind. That I must keep my eyes on You, my mind in Your Word, my feet on Your path. That I must understand, acknowledge, and believe that no matter how bad things look in the moment, You will make them good, You will put them right in the end.

When fear rears its head, Lord, come quickly to my rescue. Smother me with Your reassurances, with Your promises that You have a better way. That all I need is to believe You will do something wonderful, so far above my imagination, my expectations. That love (aka, *You*) will find a way where there seems to be no way. In Jesus' name, amen.

The Believing World

By faith, Noah built a ship in the middle of dry land. He
was warned about something he couldn't see, and acted
on what he was told. The result? His family was saved.
His act of faith drew a sharp line between the evil of
the unbelieving world and the rightness of the believing
world. As a result, Noah became intimate with God.
HEBREWS 11:7 MSG

Lord, each moment I have two choices: I can be a member of the unbelieving world or a member of the believing world. I choose the latter. Why? Because I want to be on the right path—*Your* path. In doing so, I will get to know You more and more. And the more I know You, the more I will become like You.

So here I am, Lord. A believer who looks to You and Your Word for encouragement, warning, guidance, fellowship, hope, peace, and wisdom. Give me the strength to act on what You tell me. For my doing so will not only save me, but the family with which You have gifted me. By following You, who I cannot see, I will find my way in both the visible and invisible worlds. Even better, I will be on the right track, the path of a believer, the way that leads me ever closer to You. Amen.

True to the Faith

After they proclaimed the good news there and taught
many disciples, they returned to some of the cities they
had recently visited—Lystra, Iconium, and Antioch
in Pisidia. In each place, they brought strength to the
disciples, encouraging them to remain true to the faith.

Paul and Barnabas: *We must go through many*
persecutions as we enter the kingdom of God.

ACTS 14:21–22 VOICE

No one ever said that life was going to be easy, especially the life of a believer. After all, good things are rarely easy. Thus, I pray, Lord, that You would give me all the encouragement I need each and every day, so that I will have the strength to remain true to You and to the faith.

When hardships knock at my door, when I feel as if I am drowning in doubt, when my faith is growing faint, remind me that You have not abandoned me. That You are working in my life, making a way for me to grow ever closer to You. That You are working behind the scenes to make things come out right. That You are growing me in my faith. That no matter how dark things seem, You are providing a light for me so that I can find my way to You. Amen.

Choose to Rejoice!

Though the fig tree does not blossom and there is no
fruit on the vines, though the yield of the olive fails
and the fields produce no food, though. . .there are
no cattle in the stalls, yet I will [choose to] rejoice
in the LORD. . . ! The Lord GOD is my strength [my
source of courage, my invincible army]; He has made
my feet [steady and sure] like hinds' feet and makes
me walk [forward with spiritual confidence].
HABAKKUK 3:17–19 AMP

On days when there seems no hope for this world, when I am unsure of the plan You have for my life, when nothing seems to be going right, help me shore up my faith by rejoicing in You. By remembering that no matter what happens here, my real home resides with You.

So even if the trees become barren, a crop fails, we run out of food, or the links in the supply chain grow even weaker, I am looking to You, Lord, for hope and reassurance. You are my source of calm, courage, and confidence. You are the one who gives me the strength to rise, walk, and run into Your arms.

No matter what befalls me and this world, I choose to rejoice in You—my Lord God, Savior, and King. Amen.

Open Ears

*"Behold, I stand at the door [of the church] and
continually knock. If anyone hears My voice and opens
the door, I will come in and eat with him (restore him),
and he with Me. He who overcomes [the world through
believing that Jesus is the Son of God], I will grant to
him [the privilege] to sit beside Me on My throne."*
REVELATION 3:20–21 AMP

I pray, Lord Jesus, that You will help me to overcome any doubts that are troubling me. Empty my mind of wrong-thinking, my heart of misgivings. Open my ears and spirit to Your voice.

May I always remember that You, Lord, are just on the other side of the door. That You are continually knocking, waiting for me to reach out and open up to You. And that when I do open that door, You will come in and eat with me, restoring my faith, forgiving my faults. For only with You in my life, in my home, in my heart will I be able to overcome the world.

I know in truth that You, Jesus, are the Son of God. My salvation rests in You alone. Only through coming to You and by walking Your way will I find the words to lead me to our Father. Amen.

When You Doubt

God's Promises

• •

Your kingdom is an everlasting kingdom. You
rule throughout all generations. The LORD always
keeps his promises; he is gracious in all he does.
PSALM 145:13 NLT

The Fruit of God's Promises

"So will My word be which goes out of My mouth;
it will not return to Me void (useless, without result),
without accomplishing what I desire, and without
succeeding in the matter for which I sent it."

ISAIAH 55:11 AMP

. . . .

I love Your Word, Lord, for it is filled with so many promises, all of them designed to keep me in step with You so that I may walk in rhythm with You. Your vows to those who believe and trust in Your name garner hope within, fending off doubts that attempt to pull my faith apart and aligning my will with Yours.

You, Lord, are a God of truth. And that's how I look at all the promises that have come out of Your mouth and come to fruition in the history and lives of Your people.

Help me take today's promise—that every word that has come out of Your mouth will accomplish what You desire it to—to heart. Help me etch it into my brain so that when doubts begin to assail me, I will have the weapon of Your Word to ward off any misconceptions or untruths that arise. Open my eyes and ears to the ways in which Your promises have borne fruit in my world—within and without. And my lips will give praise to You, promise by promise. Amen.

A Pursuer of the Promises

We want you all to continue working until the end so
that you'll realize the certainty that comes with hope and
not grow lazy. We want you to walk in the footsteps of
the faithful who came before you, from whom you can
learn to be steadfast in pursuing the promises of God.
HEBREWS 6:11–12 VOICE

Lord, when I feel like giving up, when I feel like it's me against the world, when the candle in my heart begins to flicker and fade, light me up with the reminder that I have inherited Your promises. They are a gift from You to me—not because I am worthy or unworthy, just because I am Your daughter.

So keep me looking up, Lord, at the bounty of Your promises. Give me an expectant attitude that You will come through, You will redeem me, You will give me strength, You will always be there for me. As I look at those who have gone before and have never given in to the world's wiles but stayed on the spiritual path, I garner new strength, new hope, new calm, and new direction. I become a pursuer of Your promises, staying steadfast in You. Amen.

Promised Holy Spirit

It's in Christ that you, once you heard the truth
and believed it (this Message of your salvation),
found yourselves home free—signed, sealed, and
delivered by the Holy Spirit. This down payment
from God is the first installment on what's coming,
a reminder that we'll get everything God has
planned for us, a praising and glorious life.
EPHESIANS 1:13–14 MSG

Lord of love, as soon as I accepted Your Son, Jesus, I was identified as belonging to You. I became a part of Your family and received Your Holy Spirit as promised. And I have never been the same since! And that's a good thing!

So, Lord, when all seems hopeless, when I am tied up in despair, when the cords of despondency begin to wrap themselves around me, remind me of who I am: Your daughter, the sister in Christ, the woman of Spirit. Help me to realize that Your gift to me of the Holy Spirit was just a down payment to what will be coming from Your hand to me. For You have planned a wonderful life for me, one in which I will see Your blessings, expect Your presence, and inherit all the other promises that await a member of Your family. In understanding this and focusing on it, not only will I be able to keep the doubts at bay but find continual praise to You bursting forth from my lips. Amen.

Choose to Believe

Elizabeth gave a glad cry and exclaimed to Mary, "God has blessed you above all women, and your child is blessed. Why am I so honored, that the mother of my Lord should visit me? When I heard your greeting, the baby in my womb jumped for joy. You are blessed because you believed that the Lord would do what he said."
LUKE 1:42–45 NLT

Oh Lord, what a wonderful speech Elizabeth gave when Mary, the soon-to-be mother of Jesus, entered her home. When the older cousin heard Mary's greeting, Elizabeth's unborn child leapt within her. She could not help but gush her blessings out upon the young girl.

What a marvelous message to all the women who would follow in the footsteps of these believers. How wonderful that women of all ages and eras found that they would be blessed because they believed God would do as He promised.

How beautiful to be blessed in simply believing! Yet how often my doubts in You or Your Word make me imagine myself cursed! Perish the thought! Lord, help me to always remember that *I will be blessed*—in this life and the next—because I believe You will stay true to Your Word. Always. No matter how many troubles and challenges come my way, I pray I will always choose to believe in You. And, in doing so, find myself blessed. Amen.

True Trust

That's why we live with such good cheer. You won't see us drooping our heads or dragging our feet! Cramped conditions here don't get us down. They only remind us of the spacious living conditions ahead. It's what we trust in but don't yet see that keeps us going.

2 Corinthians 5:6–7 MSG

Lord, I've been dragging my feet for so long, my doubts have kept me so down that I'm not sure I can get up again. But that's because I've got things turned around.

Your Word tells me that I can live a life of joy if I trust in what You have waiting for me, in what I cannot yet see but know lies at the end of this road. So I'm going to buck up, Lord! No more stumbling around in the darkness of my doubts. Instead, I'm embarking upon the pathway of trust You have set before me. I'm going to count on You, trust in Your promises, and believe that they are on their way to me and will become my reality!

That is how I will attain calm, love, kindness, blessings, and bounties that come from following hard after You. In Jesus' name I pray, amen.

The Creator's Promises

"God is not man, that he should lie, or a son of man,
that he should change his mind. Has he said, and will he
not do it? Or has he spoken, and will he not fulfill it?"
NUMBERS 23:19 ESV

. . . .

I have often been disappointed by my fellow humans, Lord. So many of them have made promises and then not followed through in the end. They either change their minds or were lying from the start. All this has made me doubt the words of those who say they will do something. So it's no wonder I sometimes have trouble believing Your promises.

Yet You, Lord, are not like humans. You are the Creator—not a creature. And if I took the time to check, I'm sure I would find in Your Word that You, the Master of infinite mercy, love, and truth, will never lie to me or change Your mind. You are so good and so honest, You may be the only person I know who will do what He says—be true to Your Word.

So forgive me, Lord, for harboring any doubts. For believing You will change Your mind, that You will speak but not act. In You, I can trust. In You, I do believe.

Because of who You are, what You have done, what You have said, I believe. And in so doing, I find my hope in and my way through Your promises. In Jesus' name, amen.

All Things

I can do all things [which He has called me to do] through Him who strengthens and empowers me [to fulfill His purpose—I am self-sufficient in Christ's sufficiency; I am ready for anything and equal to anything through Him who infuses me with inner strength and confident peace.]

PHILIPPIANS 4:13 AMP

Lord, the words of today's verse chase all uncertainties from my mind, heart, and spirit. For this promise—that I can do all You call me to do—is rooted in You and Your words. All I, the branch, must do to succeed is remain in You. You are my vine. All my strength comes from You. All I need comes from You.

You alone, Lord, give me the strength and peace that I need to keep any doubts at bay, to be the woman You created me to be, to find the power to break any barriers that may stand in my way on the path You have laid out for me.

So here I am, Lord, finding all I need in You. I am ready to move when You are. I am ready to do whatever You ask, for You will be working through me, performing all the necessary tasks, having all the pertinent know-how. With You in my life, holding my hand, working from within, speaking to my heart, walking by my side, we can do all things together. Amen.

All In

*Know this: my God will also fill every need you
have according to His glorious riches in Jesus the
Anointed, our Liberating King. So may our God
and Father be glorified forever and ever. Amen.*
PHILIPPIANS 4:19–20 VOICE

When my doubts start to rear up and leech their way into my brain, I run to Your Word, Lord. There I seek guidance, truth, and promises, anything that may vanquish my uncertainties and break their hold upon my peace, strength, and power.

As Your truths sink into my mind and heart, I realize that uncertainty has no place in my life. That I cannot and, with Your help, *will not* allow it to gain a foothold in my faith. For Your Word reminds me that I need not doubt Your help or fear any lack in my life. For You have promised that You will supply whatever I need for whatever You have called me to do. Because of Your promise to me, I can rest, knowing that what I require will come just when I need it.

So, I thank You, Lord, for supplying all I need to live this life for You, to walk in Jesus' steps. Because You are "all in" with me, giving me what I require when I require it, I am "all in" with You today and every day. Amen.

The Promise of His Presence

"When you pass through the waters, I will be with you; and through the rivers, they shall not overwhelm you; when you walk through fire you shall not be burned, and the flame shall not consume you."

ISAIAH 43:2 ESV

Speaking through the prophet Isaiah, You, Lord, promised that You would be with us when we faced floodwaters. You have promised we would not be swept away by their fierceness. Nor would we be burned by the flames when we walked through the fire.

And You proved that promise when King Nebuchadnezzar had Jewish exiles Shadrach, Meshach, and Abednego punished because they wouldn't bow down to an idol. Even before they were pushed into the fiery furnace, they told the king that no matter what he threatened, they would still bow to no one but their true God.

The miracle was that when Shadrach, Meshach, and Abednego were pushed into the fire and encountered the flames, Nebuchadnezzar witnessed a fourth figure walking around with them. And that fourth figure looked "like a son of the gods!" (Daniel 3:25 MSG).

You, Lord, have and continue to demonstrate the proof of Your promises in our lives and in those around us. I am certain of not only Your promises but Your presence when times get tough. For this and so much more, I thank You. Amen.

Commanded

"Have I not commanded you? Be strong and
courageous! Do not be terrified or dismayed (intimidated),
for the LORD your God is with you wherever you go."
JOSHUA 1:9 AMP

When preparing Joshua to take on the leadership of the Israelites, You, Lord, made sure he knew the promises You had made to Moses were now his. You told him that just as You had been present with Moses, You would be present with Joshua. Then, three times you told him to be strong and courageous (Joshua 1:6, 7, 9). Why? Because You walked with him.

Today, Lord, I take ownership of Your command to be strong and courageous. I will be unafraid and not allow myself to be intimidated. I will find the power to do this because I believe in Your promise: that You will be with me, right by my side, wherever I go.

As I walk this life in Your presence, Lord, I will not stray or allow my doubts to pull me off course. Instead, I will read and focus on Your Word. I will meditate upon it day and night. I will allow Your truths to guide me, to shield me from fears and uncertainties. For in doing so, in following Your command, I will be walking in obedience to You, my Lord, my Savior, my all. Amen.

Promised Promises

"What's more, I am with you, and I will protect you wherever you go. One day I will bring you back to this land. I will not leave you until I have finished giving you everything I have promised you." Then Jacob awoke from his sleep and said, "Surely the LORD is in this place, and I wasn't even aware of it!"

GENESIS 28:15–16 NLT

I stand amazed, Lord, at how I can have any doubt that You are right here with me. In fact, You have always been with me. You, my protector, have promised to stick with me until You have given me all that You've promised me.

May I, Lord, be as committed to You as You are to me. May I trust that You are always walking by my side. May I hold each day in Your presence as sacred. May I have open eyes and an open heart when I am walking in Your way. May I find Your light no matter how dark my path becomes. May I awaken from my sleepwalking, shake off any doubts I have been harboring, and bring all into the light of Your presence. May I acknowledge and live my life in the certainty that You are my constant companion and promised protection in every corner of this world and beyond. Amen.

No Lack

*The LORD is my shepherd; I shall not want. He
makes me lie down in green pastures. He leads me
beside still waters. He restores my soul. He leads
me in paths of righteousness for his name's sake.*

PSALM 23:1–3 ESV

You have promised, Lord, to be a faithful shepherd to Your people.
That truth is what I need to override my fear of never having enough
or never being good enough. So today, Lord, I tap into Your power
and Your promise and, in doing so, I overcome any uncertainties I
may have. I will accept as truth that You are always with me, making
sure I have what I need to do what You call me to do—even if that
call is for me to rest.

So here I am, Lord, going where You lead, knowing You will take
care of me, come what may. I rest in the knowledge that with You
alone I will experience peace. You make me brand-new, as You do
each day. You lead me in the way You would have me go so that I
will bring glory to Your name.

Oh, great and good shepherd, open my ears to Your voice, my
heart to Your love, my eyes to Your care. Amen.

God Remembers His Promise

*He spread a cloud for a covering, and fire to give
light by night. They asked, and he brought quail, and
gave them bread from heaven in abundance. He
opened the rock, and water gushed out; it flowed
through the desert like a river. For he remembered
his holy promise, and Abraham, his servant.*

PSALM 105:39–42 ESV

Lord, there is nothing You won't do to live up to the promises You have made to Your people. You bless us with Your cover of protection. You give light so that we will be able to find our way through the darkness. When we prayerfully ask for daily needs to be met, You fulfill them above and beyond what we could ever hope or imagine and in ways we never thought possible.

You, Lord, work wonders, providing water in the desert and calm amid the storm, always keeping Your people and their needs in Your mind.

Because of Your promised blessings, I am filled with peace and hope. With You in my life, with Your watchful eye upon my form, with Your supply filling whatever I may need, I do not fear anything. In Jesus' name, amen.

Promise Sent

"Listen carefully: I am sending the Promise of My Father [the Holy Spirit] upon you; but you are to remain in the city [of Jerusalem] until you are clothed (fully equipped) with power from on high."
LUKE 24:49 AMP

. . . .

Dear Lord, I praise You for all the promises You have brought to fruition, and most especially for the one You made through Your prophet Joel (2:28) where You vowed to send Your Spirit to live amid and within Your sons and daughters. It is that promise that I cling to and call on in this moment.

Lord of love, open my heart to Your Spirit's presence within me. Help me to open my ears to His voice, my heart to His urging, my feet to His ways, my mind to His words. For only when I am living in awareness of His light within me do I feel fully equipped and empowered to live a life worthy of Your calling.

God of my heart, may Your Holy Spirit so fully penetrate my being that any remaining doubts or uncertainties I have about my work and life in You flee. May I be so absorbed in His light that Your power, courage, and calm overtake my weakness, fear, and angst. Amen.

Protecting Angels

Because you have made the Lord, [who is] my refuge,
even the Most High, your dwelling place, no evil will
befall you, nor will any plague come near your tent. For
He will command His angels in regard to you, to protect
and defend and guard you in all your ways [of obedience
and service]. They will lift you up in their hands, so that
you do not [even] strike your foot against a stone.
PSALM 91:9–12 AMP

Lord, when I am cowering in place, Your Word reassures me that I am safe with You as my refuge. When I allow myself to dwell in You, when I shelter myself and those I love beneath Your wings, I know nothing can truly hurt me. For You have promised to send Your angel ahead of me, to guard me and shield me from harm as I walk upon this pathway You have laid out for me. You have promised Your angel will lead me to the place You have prepared for me (Exodus 23:20).

Open my eyes, Lord, to the angels You send into my life, to reassure and protect me, to lead me and comfort me. And may I myself act as an angel to those You put in my path, protecting them with my prayers, helping them to find their way to You. Amen.

Holding Fast Our Faith

Let us go right into the presence of God with sincere
hearts fully trusting him. For our guilty consciences
have been sprinkled with Christ's blood to make us
clean, and our bodies have been washed with pure
water. Let us hold tightly without wavering to the hope
we affirm, for God can be trusted to keep his promise.
HEBREWS 10:22-23 NLT

In this world, Lord, it is so easy for hope to turn to despair. Yet that can only happen if we forget about the many promises You have made to us.

So here I am, Lord, wavering in the way. Help me find firm footing in the assurance of Your promises. Help my faith overcome any doubts I might be entertaining. Shed Your light upon my thoughts so that the darkness of uncertainties is banished from my mind.

I want to let go of my misgivings and grab hold of the hope that comes in knowing that You, unlike most of humankind, are a man of Your Word. Your promises *will* be fulfilled in my life. For You are trustworthy, reliable, honest, and true.

Holding fast to the faith and hope I have in You, Lord, I come into Your presence, fully assured You will keep Your promises. In Jesus' name I pray, amen.

This Is What the Promise Said

*It is not the children of the body [Abraham's
natural descendants] who are God's children, but
it is the children of the promise who are counted as
[Abraham's true] descendants. For this is what the
promise said: "ABOUT THIS TIME [next year] I WILL COME,
AND SARAH SHALL HAVE A SON." And not only that, but
this too: Rebekah conceived twin sons by one man
[under the same circumstances], by our father Isaac.*
ROMANS 9:8–10 AMP

You continually amaze me, Lord. For You not only make Your children blanket promises, You make each of us an individual promise, coming down and working directly in our lives.

This removes whatever uncertainties I may have entertained in my mind and heart when it comes to how Your promises of so long ago are still relevant to me today. . .how You speak to us as Your children as a whole and on an individual basis.

You know the struggles I am currently facing in my life, Lord. And You know the path You have set me upon. So I ask You, God of my heart, to speak Your promise into my circumstances. Your doing so will give me the confidence I need to rid my mind of worry and mend the breaking of my heart. I pray You would open my ears to Your voice in the days ahead. Amen.

Not a Single One

Not a single one of all the good promises that He had
made to the house of Israel went unfulfilled; all of them
came to pass. . . . The time has come for me to die and
return to the earth. But I want to leave you with these
thoughts: Think back and you will know without a doubt
that not one single good thing that the Eternal One, your
God, promised you has been left undone. Not a single one.
JOSHUA 21:45; 23:14 VOICE

Lord, two times Joshua made sure Your people knew that not a single one of Your promises was left unfulfilled. All of them came to fruition.

You are the Lord of lords, the God of gods. You alone will leave no promise unfulfilled. These are the truths I need to impress upon my mind. For this task, I ask Your help, Lord. Continue to show me through Your Word the promises You fulfilled in the life of Your people as individuals and as a congregation. Help me to then look back in my own life and realize all the ways You have come through on Your promises to me. May I then use that as my basis for moving forward each day, knowing You will walk beside me, move within me, lead me in the way You would have me go, as all Your promises become my reality. Amen.

Promised Perfect Peace

"Peace I leave with you; My [perfect] peace I give to you; not as the world gives do I give to you. Do not let your heart be troubled, nor let it be afraid. [Let My perfect peace calm you in every circumstance and give you courage and strength for every challenge.]"

JOHN 14:27 AMP

In these troubling times, Lord Jesus, the last thing I feel is peaceful. Yet You have promised Your believers peace—a perfect peace. One that will keep our hearts from being troubled, prevent us from being afraid, and draw us closer to You.

Your peace is available to me in this moment, Lord. And to take it up, I must no longer doubt that I can access this peace. I must rid myself of the uncertainties that undermine this gift You have bequeathed to me.

So here I am, Lord, taking up this precious, promised, perfect peace. May it calm me in every circumstance and override any anxiety and angst attached to me. May Your peace give me the courage to do what You have called me to do, to boldly rise above any fears that may threaten the plan You have for me. May Your peace give me the strength I need each day for every challenge that may come my way. Amen.

Claiming the Promises

*Then Moses summoned Joshua. He said to him with all
Israel watching, "Be strong. Take courage. You will enter
the land with this people, this land that God promised
their ancestors that he'd give them. You will make them
the proud possessors of it. God is striding ahead of you.
He's right there with you. He won't let you down; he
won't leave you. Don't be intimidated. Don't worry."*
DEUTERONOMY 31:7–8 MSG

Moses faithfully led Your people through the wilderness, Lord, knowing
that You would give them the land, as promised. He knew You were
not only walking ahead of them but alongside of them, determined to
never let them down, to never leave them. Thus Moses, unlike some
other believers, never doubted You, and so he was never intimidated
and never worried.

Today I claim those same promises. In so doing, my doubts
wane and my courage rises. My steps become surer, for I affirm the
certainty that You are right here with me, even in this very moment,
looking out for me. My strength will increase each day, for it will no
longer be sapped by endless, useless fretting.

Thank You, Lord, for staying true to Your Word, for staying by
my side, for never letting me down. Amen.

The Waiting Game

*Remember when God made His promise to
Abraham? He had to swear by Himself, there being no
one greater: "Surely I will bless you and multiply your
descendants." And after Abraham had endured with
patience, he obtained the promise he had hoped for.*
HEBREWS 6:13–15 VOICE

Dear Lord, there are times when I run out of patience while awaiting the fulfillment of Your promises. That's when doubts begin to creep into my heart and mind, disrupting my spirit, wounding my soul.

I must remember that I live in a culture of instant gratification. Yet I know the truly good things always take a certain amount of time.

Help me keep in mind, Lord, that You will, in time, bless me. That if I want to obtain the promise I'm hoping for, I must patiently endure the waiting time.

I pray, Lord, that as I dig into Your Word each day, I will realize that many of Your children kept the faith as they waited for their promises to be fulfilled. Abraham himself never doubted You would keep Your Word—and he was blessed by You time and time again.

Gift me, Lord, with the blessing of patience, knowing that You will come through. All I need to do is have faith. . .and wait. Amen.

Confident Trust

So do not throw away this confident trust in the
Lord. Remember the great reward it brings you!
Patient endurance is what you need now, so
that you will continue to do God's will. Then
you will receive all that he has promised.
HEBREWS 10:35–36 NLT

There are some days, Lord, when I simply want to take another path from the one You have for me, because it feels as if I am getting nowhere.

Then I remember that I simply need to trust that You know what is best. That You will tell me when to stay put and when to move on, just as You did with the Israelites when they were wandering in the wilderness. In actuality, they were not wandering at all. They were simply following Your lead. For "Whenever the cloud lifted from over the sacred tent, the people of Israel would break camp and follow it. And wherever the cloud settled, the people of Israel would set up camp. In this way, they traveled and camped at the LORD's command" (Numbers 9:17–18 NLT).

Thus, Lord, I'm going to confidently and patiently trust You, keep my eyes on You, moving when You tell me to move, and staying put when You tell me to stay put. For in so doing, in the end—and perhaps along the way—I will be rewarded. Amen.

Time and Space

*Don't overlook the obvious here, friends. With God, one
day is as good as a thousand years, a thousand years as
a day. God isn't late with his promise as some measure
lateness. He is restraining himself on account of you,
holding back the End because he doesn't want anyone
lost. He's giving everyone space and time to change.*

2 Peter 3:8-9 MSG

. . . .

There are times, Lord, when uncertainty about my loved ones makes
my faith falter. There are some who still do not know You. And my
worries about their destination sometimes keep me up at night.

But then I come across these verses in Your Word. And I realize
that I need not worry about anything. You have it all in hand. Your
timetable is not at all the same as mine. To You, one day is like a
thousand years and a thousand years like one day.

So I leave all my worries in Your hands, knowing that You have
a plan in mind, one that I cannot completely comprehend. You, in
Your wisdom, are giving people the chance, the time and space to
change. All I need to do is know and understand that You will keep
Your promise in Your own time and in Your own way. That's Your
part. My part is to trust and wait in faith. Amen.

Committed

*"You will keep in perfect and constant peace the
one whose mind is steadfast [that is, committed
and focused on You—in both inclination and
character], because he trusts and takes refuge in
You [with hope and confident expectation]."*
ISAIAH 26:3 AMP

. . . .

Living through these troubled times has not been easy, Lord. Too
often my doubts around Your promises to me rise up, throwing my
peace to the wind.

Yet You have provided an anchor of hope within Your Word.
There I find a reminder that if my eyes would only stay focused on
You, if my heart and mind would only remain dedicated to You, then
I would regain the peace I long for. If I would trust in You, commit
to You, and place my hope in You, confident that Your promises *will*
become my reality, I would no longer have room for doubt.

So be with me now in this moment, Lord. Help me take my mind
off my what-ifs and focus on Your will-bes, knowing that in doing so,
my hope will be revived and Your peace obtainable once more. In
Jesus' name I pray, amen.

Unfaltering Eternal One

Even if the mountains heave up from their anchors, and the hills quiver and shake, I will not desert you. You can rely on My enduring love; My covenant of peace will stand forever. So says the Eternal One, whose love won't give up on you.
ISAIAH 54:10 VOICE

You, Lord, are amazing. Just as I—overwhelmed with niggling doubts—am about to give up on You and Your promises, You, who are the personification of love, promise never to give up on me!

As I watch the world and people You created go through so much upheaval, I can find my peace and rest in Your vow to never leave me. Even as hills shiver and quake, as glaciers melt and fall into the sea, as the oceans rise and threaten the shorelines, *even then* You are still in control. And I can count on Your everlasting love and promise of peace to stand sure, steady, and true.

O Eternal One, who remains faithful though I may falter, I praise Your name! I place my trust in Your promises!

As I live through these days, I pray You would continue to be my anchor, my shelter in the storm, my love amid the loveless, my peace within the chaos. Help me keep my faith in the certainty of Your promises and my mind entrenched in Your Word. Amen.

Kept Hold Of

"For I the LORD your God keep hold of your
right hand; [I am the Lord], Who says to
you, 'Do not fear, I will help you.' "
ISAIAH 41:13 AMP

O Lord my God, when I am riddled with uncertainties as to Your presence and aid in my life, remind me that You will not let me down. You will not let me falter. After all, You, the one who created me, have a plan. A *good* plan. You have created me, equipped me, and shaped me so that I can become the woman You intended me to be.

Help me, Lord, to engrave Your words upon my heart and mind. When I feel as if I am freefalling, I pray You would make it a certainty in my mind that I need not fear. You, the Lord of all, have a good grip on my right hand. And because You do, although I may stumble, You will never let me fall away from You. In fact, You will help me cross whatever threshold needs crossing, just as You made a way for the Israelites to cross the Red Sea as if they were walking on dry sand.

You are the doer of miracles. You make a way where there seems to be no way. You are my Lord and God, my help and salvation, my rock and refuge, my peace and power. I aim to keep a tight grip on Your hand. Amen.

When You Doubt

Your Influence

· ·

*You are a chosen people. You are royal priests, a holy
nation, God's very own possession. As a result, you
can show others the goodness of God, for he called
you out of the darkness into his wonderful light.*

1 PETER 2:9 NLT

Standing Firm

[Joshua and Caleb said], Don't be afraid of the land's inhabitants. It is we who will devour them! They are now defenseless, and nothing can protect them from the Eternal, who is with us. You don't need to be afraid of them! But the rest of the Israelites were not convinced. Enraged, the crowd moved to stone Joshua and Caleb.

NUMBERS 14:9–10 VOICE

Dear Lord, I don't want to be filled with doubts, to forget that You are mightier and greater than anything or anyone that may come against me. For fear is contagious, threatening to pull others away from You and who You are.

May I have the courage of Joshua and Caleb who, regardless of the power and might of their people's enemy, knew that with You, anything is possible. May I stand firm in You and Your Word, allowing both to keep me on the straight and narrow, rather than the remarks and opinions of others. May I rest in hope rather than desperation, seek to move forward in faith with You rather than backward in my own imaginings. May I encourage rather than discourage. May I become firmly entrenched in Your vision rather than my skewed sense of reality. In Jesus' name I pray, amen.

Leading with Love

*Aramean raiders had invaded the land of Israel, and
among their captives was a young girl who had been given
to Naaman's wife as a maid. One day the girl said to her
mistress, "I wish my master would go to see the prophet in
Samaria. He would heal him of his leprosy." So Naaman
told the king what the young girl from Israel had said.*

2 KINGS 5:2–4 NLT

When I begin thinking my words and actions have little effect on others, remind me, Lord, of the little girl who, even though she had been torn from her friends and family and was forced to become a servant in enemy territory, still was able to influence not only her master and mistress but kings! And she did so by simply speaking from her heart.

Just as Your Word has had such an influence over me and my own life, my words have an influence over those with whom I come in contact. So help me, Lord, to always lead with love. To spread the word of Your goodness and power. To help those who have hurt me. To have the courage to speak of You in my enemy's camp.

I pray that in so doing, my words about You would spread from mouth to mouth, from ear to ear, from simple folk to kings. In Jesus' name, amen.

Light-Bearers

"You're here to be light, bringing out the God-colors in the world. God is not a secret to be kept. We're going public with this, as public as a city on a hill. If I make you light-bearers, you don't think I'm going to hide you under a bucket, do you? I'm putting you on a light stand. Now that I've put you there on a hilltop, on a light stand—shine! Keep open house; be generous with your lives. By opening up to others, you'll prompt people to open up with God, this generous Father in heaven."

MATTHEW 5:14–16 MSG

I've sat in the darkness of doubt and uncertainty for too long, Lord. You made me to be a light-bearer. To be a beacon shining my light on the top of a hill. So it's time for me to stop hiding under a bucket.

Lord, I pray You would give me the courage to shine Your light in this world. To be generous to others, opening my arms to them in love. To forgive as I am forgiven, to love as I am loved, to shine as You shine.

Help me, Lord, to break out of this cocoon, this comfort zone I have made for myself. Give me the strength to open up to others about You, to speak Your Word, to pray on all occasions. May I simply trust in You and, in so doing, become a conduit of Your light and goodness. Amen.

The Company You Keep

Do not be deceived: "Bad company corrupts good
morals." Be sober-minded [be sensible, wake up from
your spiritual stupor] as you ought, and stop sinning;
for some [of you] have no knowledge of God [you are
disgracefully ignorant of Him, and ignore His truths].
1 CORINTHIANS 15:33–34 AMP

It's as if I have been living in a dream, Lord. Little by little, I've slipped into listening to the words and witnessing the actions of those who might be considered bad company. So I ask You, good shepherd, to pull me closer to You, back into the fold, among those who are wise in the Word, before I slip further away from You.

It is true that we "become wise by walking with the wise"; that if we hang out with fools, we'll end up watching our lives fall to pieces (Proverbs 13:20 MSG). So I pray, Lord, that You lead me to keep company with those You would consider wise and good in Your eyes. In all ways and with all people, I want to be an influencer for You. I want to spread Your love and kindness, hope and joy, peace and purpose. Amen.

A Breath of Fresh Air

Do everything readily and cheerfully—no bickering, no second-guessing allowed! Go out into the world uncorrupted, a breath of fresh air in this squalid and polluted society. Provide people with a glimpse of good living and of the living God. Carry the light-giving Message into the night so I'll have good cause to be proud of you on the day that Christ returns.
PHILIPPIANS 2:14–16 MSG

Lord, there is so much darkness in the world right now. It's hard to find common ground with friends, neighbors, and sometimes even family members. But I'm tired of hiding. So I ask You, Lord, to help me set aside my fears, my doubts, my misgivings and missteps. May I come out from my hiding place and do whatever You call me to do. May I stop balking whenever You want me to change direction.

Give me the ability to readily, cheerfully, and willingly carry Your message of love and light out into this world. Show me how to be a good example of what it means to be a godly woman, one who has risen above her own past, her own missteps, and found what it is to center herself in You. In Jesus' name I pray, amen.

Scripture's Inspired Voice

All of Scripture is God-breathed; in its inspired
voice, we hear useful teaching, rebuke, correction,
instruction, and training for a life that is right so that
God's people may be up to the task ahead and have
all they need to accomplish every good work.
2 TIMOTHY 3:16–17 VOICE

I thank You, Lord, for Your Word. For it influences me in such a way that I can become a good influence upon others.

I pray, Lord, that You would help me discipline myself to absorb more of Your Word every day. In it may I find direction, instruction, and correction. I want to live a life that is worthy of You. I want to be a good example for others.

May I allow Your Word to change me in such a way that I am continually renewed by Your power, wisdom, and grace. May the message of love I find there make me a better person—one who becomes able, willing, and equipped to do whatever You call me to do. May Your Word inspire me to inspire others, to help them bring out the best in themselves just as You bring out the best in me. Shape me, Lord, into the woman You intended me to be. Amen.

From Harmony to Chaos

A small rudder on a huge ship in the hands of a skilled captain sets a course in the face of the strongest winds. A word out of your mouth may seem of no account, but it can accomplish nearly anything—or destroy it. It only takes a spark, remember, to set off a forest fire. A careless or wrongly placed word out of your mouth can do that. By our speech we can ruin the world, turn harmony to chaos.

JAMES 3:3–6 MSG

Your Word tells me, Lord, that the words that come out of my mouth have a major influence upon the people who hear them. So I come to You, asking for guidance over what I say. Help me pause and think before I speak. Remind me that I can rely on the Holy Spirit to tell me what to say—no matter the situation.

There are so many people whose words have sparked so many fires. Words of hatred, bigotry, and chaos seem to be burning out of control. But You would have Your people, Your daughters, speak words of peace, encouragement, and love.

I pray that whatever I would say would not only be pleasing to Your ears but promote harmony in this time and place. In Jesus' name, amen.

Defined by God

If you are a woman with a husband who is not a
believer but he wants to live with you, hold on to him.
The unbelieving husband shares to an extent
in the holiness of his wife, and the unbelieving wife
is likewise touched by the holiness of her husband.
Otherwise, your children would be left out; as it is, they
also are included in the spiritual purposes of God. . . .
And don't be wishing you were someplace else or with
someone else. Where you are right now is God's place
for you. Live and obey and love and believe right
there. God, not your marital status, defines your life.
1 CORINTHIANS 7:14, 17 MSG

Lord, I ask for the assurance of Your presence in my life. And I pray that I may be an influence on those to whom I'm closest; that my loved ones would be touched by my holiness, and that I, in turn, may be touched by theirs.

I realize people—including myself—are not perfect. And that there are times when I wish my life was different. But I also realize You've put me where I am for a reason. That it's my relationship with You that defines my life. So help me, Lord, wherever I am, to live, obey, love, and believe. As I do so, I release my loved ones to You, Lord, knowing You have the best plan for all. Amen.

Digging Deep

Devote yourself to public reading [of Scripture],
to preaching and to teaching [the sound doctrine
of God's word]. Do not neglect the spiritual gift
within you, [that special endowment] which was
intentionally bestowed on you [by the Holy Spirit].
1 TIMOTHY 4:13–14 AMP

Lord Jesus, You forever changed my life. You are the light and love I have always looked for. Although there is no way to repay what You have wrought within me and my life, I can find a way to forgo any doubts and uncertainties within and find the courage and determination to spread Your good news without. Your words have the power to not only transform hearts and minds but to move mountains and irrigate deserts.

So I ask You, Lord, to help me find the time to dig deep into and explore the wonderland of Your Word. Continually use it to change me, mold me, and bring me ever closer to You. Implant within me the courage to read Your Word, to preach it, or teach it. Show me what gift You have intentionally planted within me and how I can use it so that more and more people would see Your light in me and be drawn ever closer to You.

I am Your willing servant, Lord. Work through me to whatever end You had in mind from the beginning. Amen.

Ending Well

Then they told the king, "That man Daniel, one of the captives from Judah, is ignoring you and your law. He still prays to his God three times a day." Hearing this, the king was deeply troubled, and he tried to think of a way to save Daniel.

DANIEL 6:13–14 NLT

Too often, Lord, I feel that the world is influencing me more than I am influencing it. Perhaps it just seemed easier to sit back and let the world find its own way. But that's not how You would have Your faithful follower feel.

So here I am, Lord. I want to be like Daniel who, even though it was against the law, continued to do what he had been doing—praying to You three times a day. Of course, his actions didn't change those who were against him; but it did change the king who, unable to save Daniel, was overjoyed when Daniel told him, "My God sent his angel to shut the lions' mouths so that they would not hurt me, for I have been found innocent in his sight. And I have not wronged you, Your Majesty" (Daniel 6:22 NLT).

Lord, may I, like Daniel, have an opportunity to be an influence on another soul, demonstrating to him or her that when we trust in You, all ends well in this life and the next. Amen.

Waiting with Expectation

*Be still before the L*ORD *and wait patiently for him; fret
not yourself over the one who prospers in his way, over
the man who carries out evil devices! Refrain from anger,
and forsake wrath! Fret not yourself; it tends only to evil.*
PSALM 37:7–8 ESV

It's so easy—too easy—to get upset about what's happening in the world. These days, it seems that evil too often has the upper hand. Yet the reality is that it is You, Lord, who is in control, not the chaos brought about by those who seem to delight in it.

Being upset about the actions of others or getting angry or worried about the results of their machinations does no one any good. So I come to You, Lord, asking for the strength, the faith, the patience to wait upon You in silence. I ask You to continually remind me that no matter what happens in this world, You are still in control, still watching over me, still preparing a place where I will one day live with You forever.

Instead of allowing ne'er-do-wells to influence me, to shake my faith, I will stand firm in my faith and in You. Amen.

Transformed

Do not allow this world to mold you in its own image. Instead, be transformed from the inside out by renewing your mind. As a result, you will be able to discern what God wills and whatever God finds good, pleasing, and complete.

ROMANS 12:2 VOICE

. . . .

Some days, Lord, I feel as if I am wandering in the wilderness, allowing those around me and the culture within which I am ensconced to lead me. Yet I know that this kind of wandering will keep me from entering the land of Your promise. So enough! No more of allowing the world to define me. Instead, I am coming to You in prayer, asking that You help me get closer and closer to You, allowing only You and Your Word to transform me from the inside out. I ask You to help me renew my mind in Your truths, and in that way separate myself from the falseness of this world.

In allowing You to transform me, I may then, with Your help, find a way to transform the lives of others. Then *together* we will find the wisdom to understand Your will and purpose for our lives. All to Your glory and praise! Amen.

Starlight

And many who sleep the sleep of death in the dust
of the earth will awake, some to eternal life with the
Lord and others to utter shame and eternal disgrace
far from Him. Those who are wise will shine as bright
as the sky at midday, and those who make the many
righteous will shine as the stars forever and ever.
DANIEL 12:2–3 VOICE

I know, Lord, that one day my body will die. And that You alone know when that day will be. But I pray You will help me rest in the certainty that I can shine while I'm here on earth and that when others see my light, they will see past me and catch a glowing glimpse of You.

Lord, I look forward to the day when I will spend my eternal life with You, near You. That I will shine like the stars do, forever and ever. Until then, I pray that You will help me embrace Your Word, allow its light to shine within me and, hopefully, touch the lives of all I encounter while I walk upon this earth. I pray that You will help me become more and more like Your Son, Jesus, the light of life, the light of my heart. In His name I pray, amen.

Led Astray

He had 700 royal wives, as well as 300 mistresses. And his wives and mistresses seduced his heart away from God. Solomon followed the Lord during youth and middle age, but when Solomon was an old man, these women seduced him into following other gods. His heart was led astray and no longer completely belonged to the Eternal One, his True God, as his father David's heart did.
1 KINGS 11:3—4 VOICE

I find it amazing, Lord, that Solomon, such a good and wise king, could allow himself to be led astray, away from You. It makes me wonder what is to keep me, a woman surrounded by so much temptation, on the straight and narrow path that leads to You?

Perhaps the key lies in not allowing idolatrous people and practices to seep into my worship of You. Perhaps it means taking a good look within me and around me for the little areas in which I am not giving You full rein over my life.

Not knowing all the ways the tempter could lead me to embracing little pieces of untruth, I put myself in Your protective hands, Lord. Shield me from whatever influences may cause me to stray from my path to life in You. Amen.

Influencing Others through Prayer

I urge that petitions (specific requests), prayers,
intercessions (prayers for others) and thanksgivings be
offered on behalf of all people, for kings and all who
are in [positions of] high authority, so that we may live
a peaceful and quiet life in all godliness and dignity.
1 Timothy 2:1–2 AMP

Sometimes, Lord, I feel helpless, doubting that I could in any way make things in this world better. And then I remember that You have put a powerful tool in our hands: prayer.

So, Lord, I pray that You would bless me with the determination to pray every day. That You would bring to my mind those You would have me pray for, whether they be children, parents, mayors, waitresses, moms, vice presidents, judges, or laypeople. May Your ears be open to my words. And may the Holy Spirit interpret whatever groanings and moanings I may emit in the process.

Help me, Lord, to not cross off on my prayer list any leader with whom I may not agree, as far as nationality, creed, color, age, sex, or political stance. May I pray for all people, in power and out. In return, may I find Your promised peace within and without. In Jesus' name I pray, amen.

Gathering

So let's do it—full of belief, confident that we're
presentable inside and out. Let's keep a firm grip
on the promises that keep us going. He always
keeps his word. Let's see how inventive we can be
in encouraging love and helping out, not avoiding
worshiping together as some do but spurring each other
on, especially as we see the big Day approaching.
HEBREWS 10:22–25 MSG

It's so easy, Lord, to get out of the habit of meeting with fellow believers. Yet that's not what You would have us do. You want us to be confident believers, ones who keep a firm hold on the promises You have made to us, who know that You are one who will in no way go back on His Word. Yet it can be hard to walk Your way alone.

That's why You put us in community, so that we would have a way to encourage each other, help each other, spur one another on to good deeds. So help us get back into that mindset and habit, Lord, of gathering together by whatever means possible. For we need that interaction; we need to find a way to exchange sparks of energy, the power, wisdom, and strength with which You have blessed us.

Today, Lord, I pray that You would show me at least one fellow female I might help or encourage, one whom I might inspire to continue on the path You have set before her. Amen.

Family Influence

*I remember your genuine faith, for you share the faith
that first filled your grandmother Lois and your mother,
Eunice. And I know that same faith continues strong
in you. This is why I remind you to fan into flames
the spiritual gift God gave you when I laid my hands
on you. For God has not given us a spirit of fear and
timidity, but of power, love, and self-discipline.*

2 TIMOTHY 1:5–7 NLT

Lord, thank You for the women who have put me on the pathway to You, those whose influence has kept me walking ever closer to You.

And although I have my doubts about my ability to woo anyone to You, I pray You would make me a woman open to helping others, to fanning the flames of their spiritual gifts, to leading them ever closer to You.

I pray, Lord, that You would remove from me whatever fears and reluctance I may have around influencing others to walk in Your way. Instead, I pray You would grow up in me a powerful, loving, and disciplined spirit, one that doesn't fumble with the words of her testimony or retreat into herself whenever someone asks her about her walk with You. I pray, Lord, that little by little You would build up my courage so that I can share my faith with those family members, those souls, young and old, You have gifted me. Amen.

The Holy Influencer

Deborah, the wife of Lappidoth, was a prophet
who was judging Israel at that time. . . . One day she
sent for Barak. . . . She said to him, "This is what the
LORD, the God of Israel, commands you: Call out 10,000
warriors from the tribes of Naphtali and Zebulun at
Mount Tabor. And I will call out Sisera, commander of
Jabin's army, along with his chariots and warriors, to the
Kishon River. There I will give you victory over him."
JUDGES 4:4, 6–7 NLT

I pray, Lord, that when You speak into my life, I will respond as You direct. That whatever doubts I have will fall by the wayside as I purpose to follow You. You are the greatest influence in my life, one who will bless me with the wisdom and the courage to follow Your Word, Your way, Your Spirit.

I also pray, Lord, that I would not be discouraged by those who doubt Your direction. That I would continue to work with them if that's what You require. I know You have a plan for each and every one of us. And that plan cannot in any way be thwarted by anything or anyone (Isaiah 14:27). For You will give victory where You will give victory, and You will give glory to those who deserve glory. Amen.

The Next Generation

We will tell the next generation about the glorious deeds
of the LORD, about his power and his mighty wonders.
For he. . .commanded our ancestors to teach them
to their children, so the next generation might know
them—even the children not yet born—and they in
turn will teach their own children. So each generation
should set its hope anew on God, not forgetting his
glorious miracles and obeying his commands.

PSALM 78:4–7 NLT

How will people know who You are, Lord, unless we tell them about Your deeds, wonders, and power? I pray, Lord, that You would give me the courage to stand up and teach the younger generation so that they would find their pathway to You—Your care, love, light, and provision. I also pray, Lord, that those who I teach will in turn teach the next generation so that the humans You have created will find their hope in You, would worship You above all else, and would obey Your command to love You with all their heart, soul, mind, and strength, as well as love others as themselves.

That is so what the world needs, Lord. Love, which You Yourself personify. Help me to be a part of that process. Amen.

Moving Prayers

With a prayer to the God of heaven, I replied, "If it please the king, and if you are pleased with me, your servant, send me to Judah to rebuild the city where my ancestors are buried." The king, with the queen sitting beside him, asked, "How long will you be gone? When will you return?" After I told him how long I would be gone, the king agreed to my request.

NEHEMIAH 2:4–6 NLT

It's amazing to consider, Lord, that my prayers can move You to move others. It humbles me to know that You respond to my requests even when my prayers are short SOS prayers, quick pleas in the middle of anxiety-laden moments. It blows my mind that You will, if it's in accordance with Your plans, bring out a solution and remedy a situation in ways I had never dared hope! And, for my part, all I have to do is have confidence, be certain that You hear what I say, that You will move in the best way possible, that even those of great strength, wealth, or influence are not immune to Your working on behalf of those who believe.

Help me, Lord, to be patient in the timing of Your answer to my requests. Help me to have confidence that I don't need to know exactly what Your plan is to have faith in it—and You. Amen.

Speaking Words

A soft and gentle and thoughtful answer
turns away wrath, but harsh and painful
and careless words stir up anger. . . .
A soothing tongue [speaking words that build
up and encourage] is a tree of life,
but a perverse tongue [speaking words that
overwhelm and depress] crushes the spirit.
PROVERBS 15:1, 4 AMP

It's so easy, Lord, for words to slip out of my mouth with no thought for how they will land on the ears of the hearer. Or for me to say nothing at all, which at times is even worse. For then falsehoods gain power and perhaps do just as much damage as a harsh word would have done.

What I need, Lord, what I humbly ask for is the wisdom to say the right thing at the right time. I pray You would give me the confidence to say what You are impressing upon my heart and mind. With Your soft, gentle, and thoughtful words on my tongue and with Your message, love, and light going out from my lips, anger will be stilled. The hearer's heart will be soothed, her soul encouraged, her spirit uplifted. In Jesus' name I pray, amen.

Power Prayers

Esther told them to reply to Mordecai, "Go, gather all the Jews that are present in Susa, and observe a fast for me; do not eat or drink for three days, night or day. I and my maids also will fast in the same way. Then I will go in to [see] the king [without being summoned], which is against the law; and if I perish, I perish."
ESTHER 4:15–16 AMP

Esther's story is a great reminder that God's people can have a major influence on people and world events if we can just put aside our fears and doubts and do what we are called to do.

So I ask You to give me the courage today, Lord, to do what You are calling me to do, no matter what risks may be involved. But before I do anything, Lord, I come to You in prayer, asking for protection from whatever dark powers may come up against me. I pray that You put others in my path who will join me in petitioning You for direction and wisdom. For Your Word says that where two or three are gathered together, praying in Your name, You will be in their midst. Amen.

Going God's Way

*Now the word of the LORD came to Jonah the son
of Amittai, saying, "Go to Nineveh, that great
city, and proclaim [judgment] against it, for their
wickedness has come up before Me." But Jonah
ran away to Tarshish to escape from the presence
of the LORD [and his duty as His prophet].*
JONAH 1:1–3 AMP

Dear Lord, I admit that there are times that my fears and uncertainties get the better of me. When that happens, I attempt to ignore Your voice, allowing it to be drowned out by my own thoughts. That's how I escape my purpose, the duty You have set before me. Instead of allowing You to use me to inspire, persuade, or influence others so that they will turn to You, I run the other way.

The problem is this never works out. There is no way I can escape Your presence, no way I can ignore Your influence, without it costing me more than I would like to pay.

So I come to You in this moment, Lord. Give me the courage to do what You would have me do, to go where You tell me to go, to say what You would have me say. In Jesus' name and power I pray, amen.

Getting the Best of Evil

Our Scriptures tell us that if you see your enemy hungry,
go buy that person lunch, or if he's thirsty, get him a drink.
Your generosity will surprise him with goodness. Don't let
evil get the best of you; get the best of evil by doing good.

ROMANS 12:21 MSG

I have been remiss, Lord. For I have been allowing the troubles of this world to overcome me. In allowing them to do so, I have become less of an influencer and more of an *influencee*—and not in a good way.

I confess that shortcoming now, Lord, and I ask You to give me the faith and the confidence to not allow evil to defeat me but to defeat evil by doing something good.

Today, Lord, show me how I might begin to turn myself and this world around. Tell me who I can reach out to, who I can surprise with goodness. Show me where I might shine Your light. Reveal to me the wrongs I can right by following in Your footsteps, forgiving those who have harmed me or others, and in Your name and power, overcoming their evil with Your good. Amen.

Keeping to the Script

Finally, brothers and sisters, fill your minds with beauty and truth. Meditate on whatever is honorable, whatever is right, whatever is pure, whatever is lovely, whatever is good, whatever is virtuous and praiseworthy. Keep to the script: whatever you learned and received and heard and saw in me—do it—and the God of peace will walk with you.
PHILIPPIANS 4:8–9 VOICE

You, Lord, are truth. You are the light and the way, so I am coming to You today and laying my doubts, fears, and uncertainties at Your feet. In exchange, I am taking up all the truth You reveal in Your Word.

Allow Your goodness to fill my thoughts and heart, O God. Help me to keep my thoughts on what is true, honorable, pure, and lovely. Sweep the darkness out of the recesses of my mind. Help me to keep to Your script, emulating those who have not allowed themselves to be swept up by the world's chaos and evil but have overcome it by doing right.

It is Your lead I aim to follow, Your love I live to spread, and Your goodness I long to espouse. For You alone are my God and King, my beacon of light, my rock of refuge. Amen.

Cultivating Calm

Do not even associate with a man given to angry
outbursts; or go [along] with a hot-tempered man, or
you will learn his [undisciplined] ways and get yourself
trapped [in a situation from which it is hard to escape].
PROVERBS 22:24–25 AMP

So many people are angry these days, Lord. And that's not a characteristic You would have us take on. For anger usually leads to trouble.

So, I pray, Lord, that You would give me the calm and courage I need when faced with people who are prone to angry outbursts. That You would keep me from being overwhelmed or targeted by their rage. May I instead become an immovable rock of calm, unphased by their vitriol, immune to the venom they spew, unaffected by their anger, able to keep my peace amid the storm by remaining in Your presence.

Give me the wisdom, Lord, to tear myself away from those who are hot-tempered, to sever ties with them if they will not change their ways, even if they are friends or family members. Fill me with Your peace and strength, Lord, in my effort to cultivate calm and reject rage. In Jesus' name I pray, amen.

When You Doubt

Your Future

· ·

*"For I know the plans I have for you," says
the Lord. "They are plans for good and not for
disaster, to give you a future and a hope."*

JEREMIAH 29:11 NLT

He Holds My Present and My Future

You, Eternal One, are my sustenance and my life-giving
cup. In that cup, You hold my future and my eternal
riches. . . . I will bless the Eternal, whose wise teaching
orchestrates my days and centers my mind at night. He is
ever present with me; at all times He goes before me. I will
not live in fear or abandon my calling because He stands
at my right hand. . . . You direct me on the path that leads
to a beautiful life. As I walk with You, the pleasures are
never-ending, and I know true joy and contentment.
PSALM 16:5, 7-8, 11 VOICE

Lord, when the present is arduous and the future looks bleak, I turn to You. There I find the source of my joy, strength, and song. In Your Word I find the wisdom I need to make the most of my day and to center my thoughts at night.

Knowing that You are always with me and will never leave me, I find the calm and courage I need as I walk with You through this turbulent world.

I pray that You will continue to make Your direction clear to me. That, in You, I will find never-ending pleasure, undeniable joy and contentment. Amen.

The Lord Is My Shepherd

Even though I walk through the [sunless] valley of the
shadow of death, I fear no evil, for You are with me;
Your rod [to protect] and Your staff [to guide], they
comfort and console me. . . . Surely goodness and
mercy and unfailing love shall follow me all the days
of my life, and I shall dwell forever [throughout all my
days] in the house and in the presence of the Lord.

PSALM 23:4, 6 AMP

You, Lord, have called Yourself my good shepherd, one who has already laid down Your life for me. Because You have done so, I will lay down my fear of what might come against me as I walk through the shadows of this world. Because You, the creator and sustainer of the universe, are walking by my side, holding Your rod of protection and staff of guidance, I refuse to be terrified of evil.

Lord of light, You have promised Your goodness and mercy will be with me through all my years. And in the end, You will meet with me in heaven. You, alone, are and will be my constant companion. You are the company I pledge to keep. In Jesus' name I pray, amen.

Never Forget

"I know the plans I have for you," says the Eternal,
"plans for peace, not evil, to give you a future and
hope—never forget that. At that time, you will call
out for Me, and I will hear. You will pray, and I will
listen. You will look for Me intently, and you will find
Me. Yes, I will be found by you," says the Eternal.

JEREMIAH 29:11–14 VOICE

Dear Lord, sometimes I feel so lost. I wonder if I'm actually doing Your will or just spinning my wheels. And then I turn to You and Your Word. There I find proof that You have plans for me. That those plans include peace, a future, and hope.

Remind me, Lord, that no matter where I am or what I'm doing, You will hear my voice when I cry out for You. You will listen to what I have to say. You will reveal Your presence when I seek You with all my heart, soul, and mind.

So I come in search of You now, Lord. Look down upon me. Hear the words of my prayer. Lead me to the peace and hope I long for.

Just be there. Be there and do not spare Your love. Amen.

Treasures in Heaven

*"Do not store up for yourselves [material] treasures
on earth, where moth and rust destroy, and where
thieves break in and steal. But store up for yourselves
treasures in heaven, where neither moth nor rust destroys,
and where thieves do not break in and steal; for where
your treasure is, there your heart [your wishes, your
desires; that on which your life centers] will be also."*
MATTHEW 6:19–21 AMP

. . . .

Dear Lord, it's so easy to lay up treasures here on earth, ones that
bind me to this world. Yet You tell me that moth and rust can destroy
all my earthly possessions or that the things I love could be stolen.

At the same time, Lord, You have made it clear that I should
be storing up treasure in heaven, which can never be destroyed or
stolen. Because wherever my treasure is, that's where my heart and
my life will be centered.

My truest desire is to please You, Lord. So I ask You to reveal
what You would have me stockpile in heaven. At the same time,
make clear that which You would have me let go and bless me with
the courage to do so. In Jesus' name I pray, amen.

Heavenly Home

"My Father's home is designed to accommodate all of you. If there were not room for everyone, I would have told you that. I am going to make arrangements for your arrival. I will be there to greet you personally and welcome you home, where we will be together."

JOHN 14:2—3 VOICE

Lord, worries of this world—what is happening now and what may come—keep me up at night. During the day, the news I hear keeps me wringing my hands instead of folding them in prayer.

Yet this is not the life You would have me live. So I come to You now, asking You to help me get it straight in my head that I need not worry about today or tomorrow. Instead, I need to fix my eyes on You. For You are here beside me, shielding me from harm. And when the time comes for me to leave this world, I will find a new home in Your presence.

You, Lord, have already gone ahead of me. You have prepared a home for me, one in which I will dwell with You. May I rest in that knowledge, knowing that You have planned for my future and will surely take care of the present. Amen.

Forever Guide

We pondered your love-in-action, God, waiting in your temple: Your name, God, evokes a train of Hallelujahs wherever it is spoken, near and far; your arms are heaped with goodness-in-action. Be glad. . . . Dance, Judah's daughters! He does what he said he'd do! . . . You can tell the next generation detail by detail the story of God, our God forever, who guides us till the end of time.
PSALM 48:9–11, 13–14 MSG

. . . .

You, Lord, are amazing. Each day I think about You and Your creation of wonders. I remember all that You have done for those who put themselves in Your hands. And the next thing I know, the praises to You are rolling off of my lips or are raised up in song to Your heavens.

Thank You for all the good You have brought into this world, all the light that You have shed upon Your people, illuminating their paths. I am overwhelmed by Your love and care for me. Thinking about what You have done in my life, how You have turned my heart and head around, the ways You have expressed Your kindness and showered Your goodness upon me, I cannot help but be glad. For You make good on all of Your promises.

Knowing that, I feel certain in my mind and heart that You, Lord of love, will guide me till the end of time and beyond. Amen!

His Work of Art

We are His workmanship [His own master work, a
work of art], created in Christ Jesus [reborn from
above—spiritually transformed, renewed, ready
to be used] for good works, which God prepared
[for us] beforehand [taking paths which He set],
so that we would walk in them [living the good life
which He prearranged and made ready for us].
EPHESIANS 2:10 AMP

· ·

In my eyes, Lord, I may not see myself as a masterpiece, as a work of art. Yet that's what You see when You look at me. You created me, my earthly body. Later, when I accepted You as my God, my King, my Lord and Savior, when Your Spirit touched mine, I felt myself transformed, renewed, ready for You to use me, to do what You had designed me to do.

Lord, Your Word makes clear I am here for a special purpose. So I put myself—my mind, body, strength, spirit, and soul—completely in Your hands. Set me upon the path You laid out for me so long ago. Show me which way You would have me go, what You would have me do, what You would have me say. Direct me in whatever way You desire.

Speak, Lord, for my ears are open to Your words, my mind and heart willing to serve You, here and now, in this moment. In Jesus' name, amen.

Your Name Is
Written in Heaven

Jesus said, . . . "See what I've given you? Safe passage
as you walk on snakes and scorpions, and protection
from every assault of the Enemy. No one can put a hand
on you. All the same, the great triumph is not in your
authority over evil, but in God's authority over you and
presence with you. Not what you do for God but what
God does for you—that's the agenda for rejoicing."
LUKE 10:18–20 MSG

Lord, I thank You for protecting me and shielding me from evil. I take comfort in knowing You've given me safe passage as I walk through this world and that because You are with me, no one can truly harm me. Yet I acknowledge that's not the chief joy in my life. That is reserved for the fact that it's not about what I can do for You but what You have done and continue to do for me.

I rejoice that my name is written in heaven—that I have a secure reservation to spend eternity with You—and that I am already a citizen of heaven, listed in Your book of life. I thank You, Lord, for such a wonderful promise of a fixed future forever with You. Amen.

The Spirit Friend

"When the Friend comes, the Spirit of the Truth, he
will take you by the hand and guide you into all the
truth there is. He won't draw attention to himself, but
will make sense out of what is about to happen and,
indeed, out of all that I have done and said. He will
honor me; he will take from me and deliver it to you."
JOHN 16:13–14 MSG

When the way looks hard and the future bleak, I call upon the Spirit of Truth, Lord. For You have promised that He, my Friend, will take my hand and guide me where You would have me go. He will help me make sense out of what's happening, enlighten me with Your truth, show me Your way.

I thank You, Lord, for this Spirit You have bequeathed to us. It reminds me that I am never alone, that I have a source of truth. I thank You for the fact that when I cannot find the words to pray, this Spirit can listen to and interpret all my moans and groans.

When worries about the future begin to creep into my mind, Lord, I pray that You would prompt me to seek the Spirit, to find my assurance in His presence and leading. In the name of Jesus I pray, amen.

The Moments of Life

I pour my trust into You, Eternal One. I'm glad to say, "You are my God!" I give the moments of my life over to You, Eternal One. Rescue me from those who hate me and who hound me with their threats. Look toward me, and let Your face shine down upon Your servant. Because of Your gracious love, save me!
PSALM 31:14–16 VOICE

Dear Lord Jesus, when worries assail me, when hope for the future seems dim at best, I throw myself upon You. I know that it is You alone who can save me. So I pour my trust into You.

Instead of lamenting over what might happen, I turn the moments of my life over to You, my Lord and Savior. As soon as I do so, my relief is palpable. The clouds lift, and You, the Son, shine Your love and light upon my life. I know it is You alone who can save me from whatever troubles lie ahead.

Thank You for the ways You have held me tight during difficult times. I pray that You will give me whatever wisdom I may need to face the present and the future. Knowing You are in control of me, my life, my loved ones, my world, I can rest easy. For there are no better hands to find oneself in than Yours. Amen.

Strong, Mighty, and Able

*One day the angel of GOD came and sat down
under the oak in Ophrah that belonged to Joash the
Abiezrite, whose son Gideon was threshing wheat
in the winepress, out of sight of the Midianites. The
angel of GOD appeared to him and said, "GOD is
with you, O mighty warrior!"... But GOD faced
hime directly: "Go in this strength that is yours. Save
Israel from Midian. Haven't I just sent you?"*

JUDGES 6:11–12, 14 MSG

You, Lord, have already equipped me for whatever lies ahead of me. You see me as a woman of man and a daughter of God. You see me as no other does—strong, mighty, and able. Yet I am only those things if I remember that You are with me. That You are the one who has made me strong, given me power, and designed me to do what You call me to do, to go where You send me, to serve who You would have me serve.

So instead of worrying about the future or commiserating about the present, I put myself in Your hands, Lord. I ask You to lead me wherever You will, to walk with me on the path You have already prepared. Amen.

All Along

You are still holding my right hand; You have been all along. Even though I was angry and hard-hearted, You gave me good advice; when it's all over, You will receive me into Your glory. For all my wanting, I don't have anyone but You in heaven. There is nothing on earth that I desire other than You.
PSALM 73:23–25 VOICE

Lord, when I feel all alone, when I begin to be assaulted by doubts, I look down and realize You are holding on to my hand. And even on those days when I feel I have failed You or when my future seems full of shadows, You continue to love me, protect and watch over me, and give me good advice.

I thank You for the guidance of Your Holy Spirit. When I tap into His power and feel His presence, my eyes and ears open to His promptings.

I thank You for the guidance I find in Your Word. The more I study it, the more I learn about who You are and how You work in my life. The idea that You continually hold my right hand fills me with amazement. I know I need not fear my future when You—the God of the universe—are so closely linked with me. Amen.

Such a Time as This

"Don't be fooled. Just because you are living inside the king's palace doesn't mean that you out of all of the Jews will escape the carnage. You must go before your king. If you stay silent during this time, deliverance for the Jews will come from somewhere, but you, my child, and all of your father's family will die. And who knows? Perhaps you have been made queen for such a time as this."
ESTHER 4:13–14 VOICE

You have made me a woman and placed me in this time for a specific purpose. This is what keeps me going, Lord. This is what encourages me as I prepare myself for my daily tasks. You only know what each day will bring into my life, what duty shall come to me, what blessing shall fall upon my doorstep, what challenge will appear insurmountable.

It is because I know You only mean good for me in my life that I find the courage to do whatever You call me to do. I only pray that Your direction be clear so that I can step out with confidence to take up the task before me.

For Your power, presence, and plan for me, Lord, I thank You. And now I ask, Lord, what would You have me do today in such a time as this? In Jesus' name, amen.

It's All about Trust

*Trust in and rely confidently on the Lᴏʀᴅ with all
your heart and do not rely on your own insight or
understanding. In all your ways know and acknowledge
and recognize Him, and He will make your paths straight
and smooth [removing obstacles that block your way].*
Pʀᴏᴠᴇʀʙs 3:5–6 ᴀᴍᴘ

Lord, I can wrack my brain trying to figure out all the things that might happen in these current days as well as in my future. I can even attempt to trust myself, my own wisdom, when it comes to making major decisions. But chances are, when I rely on my own judgment, I'll fall flat on my face today *and* tomorrow.

So here's what I vow to do. I'm going to trust in You, Lord, with all my heart, soul, spirit, and mind. I'm going to rely on Your insight, wisdom, and understanding. I'm going to look for You, acknowledge Your presence in my life. I'm going to listen for Your voice and follow Your promptings. For when I do these things, then and only then will You make my paths straight, removing whatever roadblocks stand in my way of living for and in You. Amen.

Why Worry?

"Give your entire attention to what God is doing right now, and don't get worked up about what may or may not happen tomorrow. God will help you deal with whatever hard things come up when the time comes."
MATTHEW 6:34 MSG

Father, You have told me in Your Word that I should not be anxious about my life because You know exactly what I need and when I need it. Just as You clothe the lilies in the field and care for the birds in the air, You will meet my needs. Your Son, Jesus, makes it clear I am more valuable than the lilies and the birds. And because You care for them in such remarkable ways, You will surely care for me.

Help me, Lord, to develop that carefree attitude You would have me maintain. Help me keep my eye on You. Prompt me not to worry about my future—what I shall eat, drink, or wear. For not only have You promised to take care of those things, but my being anxious does not, nor will it ever, add a single hour to my life.

I believe and acknowledge, Lord, that You are in control of me, my situations, my loved ones, and my future. You will not only take care of me today but during all my tomorrows. For that, I praise You! Amen.

Best Pathway

The LORD says, "I will guide you along the best
pathway for your life. I will advise you and watch
over you. Do not be like a senseless horse or mule that
needs a bit and bridle to keep it under control."
PSALM 32:8–9 NLT

Dear Lord, at times my future looks like a maze. There are so many paths that go many different directions. I find myself standing in the middle of the road, confused as to which one to embark upon.

I pray, Lord, that You would keep me from faltering at the crossroads. Remind me that Your eye is always upon me, that You are watching over me, that You will advise me as to which way to go.

Help me, Lord, not to strain against Your guidance. Help me to not be stubborn or rebellious when You try to steer me in the right direction. Help me to trust You for my future, to obey Your leading, to surrender my will to Yours. I know You have a part for me to play in Your plan. You see how all events and lives interconnect. You know what's good for me on earth and in heaven, today and tomorrow, in this moment and the next. Amen.

Confident about God

We are confident that God is able to orchestrate
everything to work toward something good and
beautiful when we love Him and accept His
invitation to live according to His plan.
ROMANS 8:28 VOICE

I have confidence that You will make something good out of everything that happens to me. I am convinced that You are able to do so from the story of Joseph. His brothers had stripped him of his colorful coat, stuck him in a pit, then sold him to some traders and told their father that Joseph was dead. The next thing he knew, he'd been sold into servitude to Potiphar, an Egyptian officer of Pharaoh's, falsely accused of rape, and committed to the king's dungeons.

Even though Joseph had been treated badly and been betrayed by his brothers, then sold into service in a foreign country, You stayed with him. And because You were with him, he prospered at whatever he set his hand to, so much so that Joseph soon became second in command and power to only Pharaoh himself!

Lord, although it may be difficult for me to endure the hard times, knowing that You are and will be with me, conducting me as I face each challenge, gives me peace, strength, and power every moment. Amen!

At Home with the Lord

So we are always of good courage. We know
that while we are at home in the body we are away
from the Lord, for we walk by faith, not by sight. Yes,
we are of good courage, and we would rather be
away from the body and at home with the Lord.

2 CORINTHIANS 5:6–8 ESV

Dear Lord, out of the body and home with You. Now that's a wonderful future! It is a promise that means I don't have to fear death. For I know that the moment I breathe my last breath, I will be home, in Your presence, cradled in Your arms.

I know that You have prepared a place for me in heaven. The thought of being there with You for eternity and what that experience will be like defies my imagination. No tears. No pain. No sorrow. What more could I want, ask, or hope for?

Knowing this fallen world is not my home helps me cope with my life here on earth. Knowing that I am here as a stranger and a foreigner somehow makes things easier. Knowing that You are with me as I walk upon this mortal coil by faith and not sight makes me less lonely and more determined to do right in Your eyes.

Remind me, Lord, of my future with You centered in my mind and heart. In Jesus' name I live and pray, amen.

Held by His Hand

The steps of a [good and righteous] man are directed
and established by the Lord, and He delights in his way
[and blesses his path]. When he falls, he will not be hurled
down, because the Lord is the One who holds his hand
and sustains him. . . . For the Lord. . .does not abandon
His saints (faithful ones); they are preserved forever.

Psalm 37:23–24, 28 AMP

Dear Lord, I don't have to worry about my future because You are directing my path. Because I am right with You, You are giving me strength for the journey. Because You are pleased with me, I know I won't trip up. But if I do stumble, I know I won't go down all the way because You are holding me by the hand, keeping me on my feet, getting me back on the right track, forgiving me where I need forgiveness.

With these kinds of promises and guarantees, I am full of comfort, confidence, and calm. My mind is at ease no matter what this world will throw my way. For nothing can keep me down when You lift me up. In You alone I find my feet, my heart, my home, my way. Amen.

Soaring High

The LORD is the everlasting God, the Creator of all the earth. He never grows weak or weary. No one can measure the depths of his understanding. He gives power to the weak and strength to the powerless. Even youths will become weak and tired, and young men will fall in exhaustion. But those who trust in the LORD will find new strength. They will soar high on wings like eagles. They will run and not grow weary. They will walk and not faint.

ISAIAH 40:28–31 NLT

I may not know exactly what's going to happen tomorrow, Lord, but I do know that You will be with me to handle whatever needs to be handled. Because You, the creator of all the earth, are in my life, I will find all the power and strength I need to walk in Your way and will. Because I trust in You with all my heart, soul, spirit, and mind, I will not succumb to exhaustion. I will not allow this world to pummel me or make me faint with worry. Instead, in You, I will surmount whatever challenges arise or obstacles block my path. For You will give me the wings of the eagle, allowing me to rise above all—but You. In You, I find my way. Amen.

Fulfill All Your Plans

May the Eternal's answer find you, come to rescue
you, when you desperately cling to the end of your
rope. May the name of the True God of Jacob be
your shelter. May He extend hope and help to you
from His holy sanctuary and support you from His
sacred city of Zion. . . . May He grant the dreams of
your heart and see your plans through to the end.

PSALM 20:1–2, 4 VOICE

Eternal God, when I wonder about my future, one thing is clear in my mind: if I find trouble—or if trouble finds me—You will help me and support me. Thus, I need not fear anything, for I am confident You will respond to my cry and overcome whatever forces battle against me.

At the same time, You know the dreams I harbor in my heart. You know the many plans I have for my future. So I pray, Lord, that You will help me align my plans with Your plans for me. The last thing I want to do is head down the wrong path. I would much rather be walking where You would have me walk, doing what You would have me do, serving where You would have me serve. My greatest desire is to have my plans be in sync with Yours. Amen.

And So It Will Be

Things will happen as I plan. Things will be as I
determine. . . . Because I, God of earth and heaven,
have devised a plan for the whole earth; I have reached
out and am ready to effect change. . . . And who can
argue with that or stand in God's way? The Eternal,
Commander of heavenly armies, has determined
that this is how it should be. And so it will be.
ISAIAH 14:24, 26–27 VOICE

It is simply amazing to know that You, Lord God, not only have a plan for me but for everyone and everything in the earth. You have already reached out and are preparing to do something now to change the status quo.

Although I sometimes have trouble with change in my life, in my world, I trust You. You know what's best not only for me but for this world. Lord, I know You have a predetermined agenda. And the last thing I want to do is get into a debate about it with You or, even worse, stand in Your way. For what You say goes. What You intend to do becomes reality.

And so I ask You to help me adjust to whatever change You are bringing into my family, my life, my world. As You move, as You speak, may I respond with "And so it will be." Amen.

Wait and See

*When Ruth returned to Naomi's home, her
mother-in-law asked her daughter what happened.
Ruth related all that Boaz had said and done. . . .*

Naomi: *Now you must wait, daughter. We must
wait and see what happens. Be at peace. That
man will not rest today until this is resolved.*
RUTH 3:16, 18 VOICE

I realize, Lord, that there will be times when questions remain unanswered, decisions are waylaid, matters are unsettled. Help me in those days to be patient, to not take things into my own hands, to not force solutions. Help me to realize that no matter how many days, weeks, months, years I have to wait, You and I will remain close and connected. My future, my hopes, my dreams, my desires, my beginning, and my end are all tied up in You.

I pray for not only patience, Lord, but for peace amid the patience. Assure me that You, who knows what's best for me, are waiting with me. If You can stay calm, I can stay calm by focusing on You, on who You are, and on the plans You have made for my present and my future.

I wait patiently and peacefully to see what will happen, knowing You have good in mind for me above and beyond what I could ever hope or imagine. Amen.

The Lord's Purpose

*He who hurries with his feet [acting impulsively
and proceeding without caution or analyzing the
consequences] sins (misses the mark). . . . Many
plans are in a man's mind, but it is the LORD's
purpose for him that will stand (be carried out).*

PROVERBS 19:2, 21 AMP

I have sometimes given in to my impulses, Lord, jumping into a situation I should have never gotten myself involved in. The next thing I know, the folly of my actions is made clear, and I spend the remainder of my time and energy trying to extricate myself from what I've created.

Lord, I pray You would help me to be a better planner. To think things out before I commit myself to anything or anyone. To consider the consequences of what I feel led to do.

Show me, Lord, how to not get so caught up in the doing that I forget to be still and acknowledge Your will and way in every planning process. Help me to remember that no matter how much brainstorming I do, no matter what strategies I come up with, it is ultimately Your purpose for me that will prevail. Help me find a way to allow You alone to not only drive but steer me on whatever route You want me to take, knowing that Your way is always the best way. In Jesus' name I pray, amen.

Taking a Stand

Moses said to the people, "Do not be afraid! Take your stand [be firm and confident and undismayed] and see the salvation of the LORD which He will accomplish for you today; for those Egyptians whom you have seen today, you will never see again. The LORD will fight for you while you [only need to] keep silent and remain calm."
EXODUS 14:13—14 AMP

Your Word makes clear, Lord, that there will be times in the future when it will be You who fights the battle and I am to stand aside. So I ask You, eternal one, to give me discernment to know when You want me to stand my ground and watch You work and when You want me to roll up my sleeves and step into the fray. If I am to stand and watch, give me the courage and confidence to wait while You defeat whatever forces have come against me. Remind me in that moment that after You have overcome the enemy, I will never see them again.

Lord, I also ask that You cover me with a curtain of calm and comfort as I keep quiet and watch You work for my good, keeping in mind that You will bring an end to those against me in ways that I could never imagine. Amen.

Doing Good

*There has never been the slightest doubt in my
mind that the God who started this great work in
you would keep at it and bring it to a flourishing
finish on the very day Christ Jesus appears. . . .
So let's not allow ourselves to get fatigued doing good.
At the right time we will harvest a good crop if we don't
give up, or quit. Right now, therefore, every time we get
the chance, let us work for the benefit of all, starting
with the people closest to us in the community of faith.*
PHILIPPIANS 1:6; GALATIANS 6:9–10 MSG

I am humbled, Lord, that You find me worthy to serve You and that every day You will continue Your great work through me.

All I ask is that You give me the strength to do what good I can in this world. Give me the power to work for the benefit of all people, beginning with my community of faith.

Draw me to Yourself in this moment, Lord. Empower me for what good You would have me perform today. Give me the courage to do what You would have me do, to persevere in whatever task You assign, knowing that all I do is for Your glory, not mine. Amen.

When You Doubt

God Hears You

· ·

I began to panic so I yelled out, "I'm cut off.
You no longer see me!" But You heard my cry
for help that day when I called out to You.
PSALM 31:22 VOICE

Set Apart for God

You can be sure of this: The LORD set apart the godly for
himself. The LORD will answer when I call to him. . . .
"He is ready to hear those who worship him and do
his will". . . . "The eyes of the LORD watch over those
who do right, and his ears are open to their prayers."
PSALM 4:3; JOHN 9:31; 1 PETER 3:12 NLT

Lord, I love the assurance that You have set aside for Yourself those who are godly. That we who worship You, who do right, who follow Your will and way are the ones You watch over. That Your ears are open to our prayers.

So I pray in this moment, Lord, that You will help me stay true to the pathway You have set out for me. That You will pull me back to You if and when I begin to stray. And when I falter, I pray that You will speak to me through Your Word so that I can lift myself back up and set things right—in Your eyes.

Hear me now, Lord, as I unburden myself to You. Answer my pleas. Hold me in Your arms now and forever as we walk in sync. Amen.

Remarkable Confidence

*This is the [remarkable degree of] confidence which we
[as believers are entitled to] have before Him: that if we
ask anything according to His will, [that is, consistent
with His plan and purpose] He hears us. And if we
know [for a fact, as indeed we do] that He hears and
listens to us in whatever we ask, we [also] know [with
settled and absolute knowledge] that we have [granted
to us] the requests which we have asked from Him.*

1 JOHN 5:14–15 AMP

I come before You, Lord, wanting to pray in accordance with Your
will. So I ask You to illuminate my mind, bless me with wisdom to
follow Your way, and pour upon me the strength I need to navigate
this world. I ask You, Lord, to open up my heart to Your truth. Help
me to engrave Your Word into my mind so that in times of trouble,
I will have a guiding light to see me through.

Lord, remind me to seek You above and beyond all else. Help
me to develop a constant awareness of Your presence beside me,
Your Spirit deep within.

Thank You for listening to my pleas, working in my life, and
answering this prayer. Amen.

Hear My Prayer, O Lord

*My heart was hot within me. While I was musing the fire
burned; then I spoke with my tongue. . . . "My hope [my
confident expectation] is in You. . . . Hear my prayer, O
L*ORD*, and listen to my cry; do not be silent at my tears; for
I am Your temporary guest, a sojourner like all my fathers."*

PSALM 39:3, 7, 12 AMP

· ·

I know, Lord, that it's not good to swallow my sorrow, my troubles, to keep from You what I need. So I come to You now, Lord. In You alone I have hope. From You alone I expect an answer. So hear me now, Lord, as I unburden myself to You. Listen to the words I speak. See the tears I'm shedding. And respond with loving-kindness to what I have to say.

I know, Lord, that I am a stranger here on this earth. That my true home is in You. So I ask You to hear my knock upon the door of Your heart. Open Your ears to the words of my prayer. Come quickly to give me relief, to spread Your peace upon me, to infuse me with strength so that I can once more rejoice in Your name and spread Your fame. In Jesus' name I pray, amen.

The Why Questions

The two children struggled with each other in her womb. So she went to ask the LORD about it. "Why is this happening to me?" she asked. And the LORD told her, "The sons in your womb will become two nations.". . . And when the time came to give birth, Rebekah discovered that she did indeed have twins!

GENESIS 25:22–24 NLT

. . . .

You, Lord, have been answering the prayers of Your people since time began.

Your book of Genesis reminds me that Isaac prayed for his wife, Rebekah, to become pregnant. And because Isaac was a believer in and follower of You, You granted his request.

Then Rebekah followed her husband's lead when she became concerned about the children within her womb. In Your Word we find the first recorded instance of a woman coming to You in prayer as she asks the age-old question: "Why is this happening to me?"

So, Lord, I come to You now, just as Rebekah did. Help me to understand what is happening. Illuminate my mind and heart so that I can deal with the situations I find myself in. Lead me to Your Word so that I can learn to be a better woman, prayer, follower, worshiper of You. Help me get it in my head that if I need answers, it is to You, my Father, that I, Your daughter, should come. In Jesus' name, amen.

Eyes on God

*"We are powerless against this great multitude which is
coming against us. We do not know what to do, but our
eyes are on You." . . . Then in the midst of the assembly
the Spirit of the L*ORD *came upon Jahaziel. . . . "The
L*ORD *says this to you: 'Be not afraid or dismayed at this
great multitude, for the battle is not yours, but God's.' "*

2 CHRONICLES 20:12, 14–15 AMP

I come to You today, Lord, confused, full of doubt and uncertainty,
yet knowing that in Your presence I will find relief, comfort, and
clarity. I humbly admit to You that I have no idea how to face what's
coming. I feel powerless in these moments, not knowing what to do.
But I do know who to run to: You.

So I'm keeping my eyes on You, Lord. For I know that You are
the one—the only one—who can lead me the way I should go, teach
me what I need to know, prepare me for what is coming, defend me
better than any physical fortress or armor.

Speak to me now, Lord. Fill me with courage. Give me the certainty that You will go before me, stand with me, protect me from
evil. In this world—and the next. Amen.

God-Awakened

The Lord GOD. . .awakens Me morning by morning,
He awakens My ear to listen as a disciple [as One
who is taught]. . . . The earth, O LORD, is full of Your
lovingkindness and goodness; teach me Your statutes.
ISAIAH 50:4; PSALM 119:64 AMP

Help me, Lord, to make seeking You a priority in my life. To that end, I ask You to awaken me in the mornings so that I can get in quality prayer time with You before my feet hit the floor. Once the kids are up, the phone starts to ring and emails ding, the dog needs to be walked or the cat fed, I want to be in Your presence. There I pray You would teach me what You would have me know. Open my ears to Your voice. Open my eyes to Your Word.

Give me a new perspective, Lord. Instead of seeing the earth as evil, harmful, and myself helpless, I ask that You remind me that although some evil lurks in the shadows, there is still an abundance of Your loving-kindness and goodness all around me.

Awaken me, Lord, to Your presence, Your moving, Your heart, Your Spirit. Show me what I can do to promote Your love and light. Work within me to shape me into the woman You created me to be. Amen.

Cry for Help

*Hear me, O Eternal One, hear my prayer! Hear my
lonely desperate cry for help. Do not hide from me
when my days are filled with anguish; lend Your ear
to my wailing, and answer me quickly when I call.*

PSALM 102:1–2 VOICE

. . . .

When my heart is filled with doubts, when my spirit needs Your immediate attention, when I am crying out to You from a place of desperation, hear my prayer, Lord! Answer me quickly when I call out to You!

Remind me, Lord, that when I cannot hear Your voice, when I feel as if You are hidden from me, it is not You who have closed Your ears or gone into hiding, it's me! I am the one who has moved away from this relationship.

So, here I am, Lord, running back to You. I am in dire straits, frantically seeking Your face, needing Your peace, provision, and power.

Hear my groans, my disjointed thoughts, my cry for help. I'm holding on to my hope in You, holding on for dear life! Show Your face, Lord. Point me to Your Word. Lead me up out of this pit of despair and into Your waiting arms. To You I run; in You I trust. In Jesus' name, I pray. Amen.

Two-Way Street

*Listen to my words, O Lord, consider my groaning
and sighing. Heed the sound of my cry for help, my
King and my God, for to You I pray. In the morning,
O Lord, You will hear my voice; in the morning I
will prepare [a prayer and a sacrifice] for You and
watch and wait [for You to speak to my heart].*
PSALM 5:1–3 AMP

Too often, Lord, I seem to forget that prayer is a two-way street. That I am to not only unburden myself to You but to watch and wait for how You respond, what answer You provide.

I ask You for Your forgiveness each time I forgot or just didn't bother to wait around to hear Your voice or feel Your touch. I ask You to remind me to reorder my prayer time so that I not only have ample time to tell You what's on my mind and heart but enough time to wait upon You.

In those waiting-for-answers moments, Lord, I ask You to open my ears to Your voice. Prompt me to seek Your response by reading and studying Your Word. Help me, Lord, to see You not as just priest, prophet, and king but as friend, beloved, and counselor. Amen.

From Problem to Promise

God said, "I've taken a good, long look at the
affliction of my people in Egypt. I've heard their cries
for deliverance from their slave masters; I know all
about their pain. And now I have come down to help
them, pry them loose from the grip of Egypt, get them
out of that country and bring them to a good land with
wide-open spaces, a land lush with milk and honey."
EXODUS 3:7–8 MSG

Dear Lord, I am encouraged when I read in Your Word that You heard Your people crying out in Egypt. You then took a good look at what was happening to them, and You knew all about their pain.

Yet You didn't stop there. You came up with a solution and began implementing a way to pry Your people from the hands of Pharaoh. Even better, You came up with a promise, something that may have been beyond their imagination: a beautiful lush land with wide-open spaces!

Because of all these things, Lord, I have the assurance that You hear my voice when I cry out to You. You take a good look at what's happening in my life. You are familiar with the pain I am experiencing. And You come up with a solution, implement a plan, and bring me into a land of promise. What more could a daughter of God want? Amen.

Hear My Words

I am praying to you because I know you will answer,
O God. Bend down and listen as I pray. Show me
your unfailing love in wonderful ways. By your
mighty power you rescue those who seek refuge from
their enemies. Guard me as you would guard your
own eyes. Hide me in the shadow of your wings.
PSALM 17:6–8 NLT

Dear Lord, when I visualize You, the God of all creation, bending down Your ear to me, listening as I pray, I am overcome with amazement. I am so thankful that I serve You—a living God who is not only interested in what I say but loves me in so many different ways.

I pray to You today seeking Your strength, wisdom, and peace. I long for Your love that, unlike human love, never fails.

Guard me today from whatever evils are lurking in the shadows. Protect me as You would the pupil of Your eye. Hide me in the protective shadow of Your wings.

I can rest in the knowledge that You hear and answer my prayers. For You are my eternal rock, refuge, wisdom, knowledge, protector, shield, comfort, and beloved God. With You in my life and heart, I am in need of no one and nothing else. Amen.

Accepted Prayer

Be gracious to me, O Lord, for I am languishing;
heal me, O Lord, for my bones are troubled. My
soul also is greatly troubled. . . . The Lord has
heard my plea; the Lord accepts my prayer.
PSALM 6:2–3, 9 ESV

Dear Lord, sometimes I wonder if You really hear my prayers. For, at times, You seem so distant.

Yet that uncertainty, those doubts, flee when I read Your Word. The psalmist tells me You hear my cry. Even when I am in deep distress, when I cry myself to sleep, You hear the sound of my weeping. . . and You act, as any good father would.

I thank You, Lord, that there is no special formula or language I need to memorize when I come to talk to You. You make my coming to You so easy. Perhaps that's why You tell us to pray to You without ceasing. To give thanks to You no matter what situation we're in. To not suppress the Spirit that resides within us. That doing all these things is Your will for us (Thessalonians 5:17–19).

Help me, Lord, to come to You with everything in prayer. And I will praise You, not only because You are interested in how I'm doing, but because You are so accepting of me and what I bring. In Jesus' name, amen.

SOS Answered!

"I called out of my trouble and distress to the LORD,
and He answered me; out of the belly of Sheol I cried
for help, and You heard my voice. For You cast me
into the deep, into the [deep] heart of the seas, and the
currents surrounded and engulfed me; all Your breakers
and billowing waves passed over me. . . . When my
soul was fainting within me, I remembered the LORD,
and my prayer came to You, into Your holy temple."
JONAH 2:2–3, 7 AMP

Lord, when I consider Jonah, his lack of faith and his blatant disobedience landing him in the belly of a whale, I take away a measure of hope. Knowing that You answered a person who ran from Your commands, my own doubts flee.

No matter what trouble I land in or how I got there, when I cry out for Your help, You will not only hear me but respond. When my life seems to be fading away, slipping through my fingers, I will remember You, come to You, pray to You. And that prayer, those words, my mumblings, moanings, and groanings will rise up all the way to Your holy heavenly temple. You will hear my prayer. You will answer my plea. You will reach down, remove the seaweed from around my head, and lift me up onto dry land. For You are my Lord. You are my rescuer. Amen.

The Helper Alongside

The moment we get tired in the waiting, God's Spirit is right alongside helping us along. If we don't know how or what to pray, it doesn't matter. He does our praying in and for us, making prayer out of our wordless sighs, our aching groans. He knows us far better than we know ourselves, knows our pregnant condition, and keeps us present before God. That's why we can be so sure that every detail in our lives of love for God is worked into something good.
ROMANS 8:26–28 MSG

I sometimes doubt, Lord, that I can learn how to pray constantly, that You hear my words, that they reach Your ears. And then I read today's verses in Your Word, and my doubts are wiped away.

Your Spirit, Lord, is always working alongside of me, helping me get through every moment. When I cannot put my pain into words, when all I can do is cry or sigh in despair, the Spirit comes up with a prayer and presents it to You.

It's not for me to know or try to figure out how the Spirit does what He does for me, for You. But it is up to me to accept it, believe it, and base my prayer life upon it—to understand that You hear about, respond to, and order every detail in my life, combining all You can to work something out for my good. To Your glory and praise, amen!

Before They Call

*While I was still speaking in prayer and extremely
exhausted, the man Gabriel. . .came to me. . . . He
instructed me and he talked with me and said, "O
Daniel, I have now come to give you insight and
wisdom and understanding. At the beginning of
your supplications, the command [to give you an
answer] was issued, and I have come to tell you, for
you are highly regarded and greatly beloved."*

DANIEL 9:21–23 AMP

Lord, You said through Isaiah (65:24 AMP), "Before they call, I will answer; and while they are still speaking, I will hear." This seems impossible for me to believe, a concept too loving for me to grasp. But then in Your book of Daniel, I see the proof of Your promise.

You, Lord, respond to us from the moment we say, "O Lord." While we are still speaking, while we are still in the midst of crying out to You, You are on the move, commanding Your angels to remind us of Your love and regard for all of those who walk Your way, directing Your servants to bring us an answer.

You have made a believer out of me, Lord. You had me at the words "greatly beloved." For this and so much more, I praise You. Amen.

He Delivered Me

*When I needed the Lord, I looked for Him; I called
out to Him, and He heard me and responded. He
came and rescued me from everything that made me so
afraid. . . . This poor soul cried, and the Eternal heard
me. He rescued me from my troubles. . . . Taste of His
goodness; see how wonderful the Eternal truly is. Anyone
who puts trust in Him will be blessed and comforted.*
PSALM 34:4, 6, 8 VOICE

Dear Lord, sometimes my doubts keep me from calling out to You.
For I fear You won't really hear my prayers, You won't understand
my problems, or You'll figure that if I got myself into a conundrum,
I should be able to get myself out.

Yet none of that is who You are or what You do. You have promised that when I need You, when I look for You and call out to You,
You will hear and respond. You will come and give me aid, rescue
me from all I fear, pull me up out of whatever trouble has me neck-
deep in mud.

Lord, You are not only the most powerful but the most wonderful
God. When I put all my faith and confidence in You, when I believe
and trust that You will come when I call, then I find the blessings
and comforts that will give me such relief, I must cry out in joyful
praise of You. Amen.

Beyond Imagination

*The Eternal who made the earth, who formed and
fashioned it, the One whose name is the Eternal, has
this to say: Call to Me, and I will answer you. I will
tell you of great things, things beyond what you can
imagine, things you could never have known.*
JEREMIAH 33:2–3 VOICE

Dear Lord, You are the master of all creation, all that is seen and unseen. You, who formed and fashioned all, have promised that if I call to You, You will answer me. And You will tell me of amazing, wonderful, great things beyond anything I could ever imagine or ever know.

It is this idea, that You, the one who knows all and sees all, the one who sustains and maintains everything, are willing to not only hear my prayers but answer my questions, help me to understand, fill me with knowledge—knowledge that no one else could possibly know.

The willingness of such a powerful, supernatural God to help out a daughter (of which He has many) staggers my imagination. Yet deep within, I know it's true. And I cannot help but praise Your name because of it! Amen.

He Inclined His Ear to Me

*I love the LORD, because He hears [and continues
to hear] my voice and my supplications (my pleas,
my cries, my specific needs). Because He has
inclined His ear to me, therefore I will call on Him
as long as I live. . . . Return to your rest, O my soul,
for the LORD has dealt bountifully with you.*

PSALM 116:1–2, 7 AMP

Dear Lord, I love You. You sent Your only Son to bear the weight of the sins of the world, mine included. You snatched me from the snares of death when You rose from the grave, conquering death and Satan. And You have heard my voice. When I shed tears upon my pillow, when my voice, small and shaky, makes pleas to Your heart, You are touched. Hearing my cries for mercy, for help, for encouragement, for love, for compassion, You reach down from the heavens and dry my eyes. And my soul can then return to its rest.

Lord of love, You hear and answer prayers. Thus, I will call on You for as long as I live. For You who are faithful, gracious, and merciful have done and will continue to do great and mighty things in my life. Amen.

Praying from the Heart

Hannah was in deep anguish, crying bitterly as she prayed to the LORD. . . . "I have been praying out of great anguish and sorrow." . . ."I am the very woman who stood here several years ago praying to the LORD. I asked the LORD to give me this boy, and he has granted my request."

1 SAMUEL 1:10, 16, 26–27 NLT

Lord, I come to You with my whole heart. To You I bear my anguish and sorrow. When bitter tears come coursing down my face, I think of how many women before me have come to You and poured out their souls, seeking mercy, grace, and strength.

May I push aside all my doubt and know with certainty that You will answer my request just as You have done for so many women in the past. For only You can do the impossible. Only You can grant my petition. Only You can lift me from the darkness and into Your light.

I know You hear my prayer, Lord, and will look upon me with compassion. So I put my broken heart in Your hands. I ask You to mend me, hold me, love me, heal me, make me whole once more. In Jesus' name I pray, amen.

Prayers Offered Up

GOD, come close. Come quickly! Open your ears—it's
my voice you're hearing! Treat my prayer as sweet
incense rising; my raised hands are my evening prayers.
Another Angel. . .was given a great quantity of incense so
that he could offer up the prayers of all the holy people
of God on the Golden Altar before the Throne. Smoke
billowed up from the incense-laced prayers of the holy
ones, rose before God from the hand of the Angel.
PSALM 141:1–2; REVELATION 8:3–4 MSG

I come to You, Lord, seeking Your presence. I pray You would come alongside of me so that I can sense Your nearness, hear Your heartbeat, feel Your breath upon my face.

Hear my trembling voice, Lord. As I raise my hands to You, I ask You to treat my prayer as an offering akin to the smoke of sweet incense rising up to Your throne, wafting around Your altar.

Your Word has assured me that You will hear me when I pray, when I call on You for help. So, as I enter Your presence, Lord, I know You will listen to what I have to say. You will help me shape my prayers so that they align with Your will and way. At the same time, Lord, continue to transform me into the woman You designed, the one You had in mind from the beginning of time. Amen.

More Inspiration for
Your Beautiful Soul

 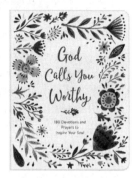

God Calls You Forgiven
978-1-64352-637-9

God Calls You Worthy
978-1-64352-474-0

These delightful devotionals—created just for you—will encourage and inspire your soul with deeply rooted truths from God's Word. Each devotional reading will assure you that God's Word is unchanging and will help you to grow in your faith as you become the beautifully courageous woman the heavenly Creator intended you to be!